With All
Good Wishes

from

Graham Clarke

1997

Tournesols Vincent. 1988. Hand coloured etching, 34.4 × 27.2 cm (13½ × 10¾ in)

Graham Clarke's

GRAND TOUR

Presenting sundry Etchings
Drawings Verses and Critical
notes concerning the Cultural
curiosities of certain parts
of France & Italy observed
& executed in the Anachronological
mode by a person of considerable
Gorm

PHAIDON · OXFORD

Phaidon Press Limited, Musterlin House, Jordan
Hill Road, Oxford, OX2 8DP

First published 1989
© Phaidon Press Limited 1989
Text and pictures © Graham Clarke 1989

A CIP catalogue record for this book is available
from the British Library

ISBN 0 7148 2571 9

Etchings published by the artist and distributed
by C.C.A. Galleries of London in editions
of 400.

Watercolours taken from Graham Clarke's
sketchbooks.

Black and white line drawings and hand
lettering created specially for the *Grand Tour*.

Printed in Great Britain by The Roundwood
Press Limited, Kineton, Warwickshire

For Jason Abigail
Emily Tilly and
Their Mum without
whom I'd have been
off on my Grand Tour
a bit sooner but
would not have had
nearly so much to
come home for.
With Love

CONTENTS

Chianti Dante. 1989. Hand coloured etching, 34.8 × 27.2 cm (13¾ × 10¾ in)

foreword

In all the long and distinguished history of the Grand Tour, it can safely be said that there was never one quite like this. But then there was never anyone quite like Graham Clarke. Having read – if that's the word – and hugely enjoyed his *History of England*, and having heard that he was now turning his attention to France and Italy, I found myself wondering how well that quintessentially English eye would survive the Channel crossing; but I need not have worried. The journey here recorded has borne fruit in abundance. The result is the astonishing volume that you now hold in your hands.

To say that it defies analysis would be an understatement. Neither picture book, guide book nor novel, neither poetry nor prose, it answers well to the description so felicitously penned by the author in his subtitle but not, I think, to any other. Apart from Michelangelo and Shakespeare – who go, of course, without saying – scholars might detect influences of Edward Lear or Osbert Lancaster, Beachcomber or the Goons, Rowland Emmett or Heath Robinson; as a traveller, however, Mr Clarke reminds me more than anyone else of Thomas Coryate, who between May and September 1608 walked to Venice and back – on his return hanging up his shoes in his parish church at Odcombe in Somerset and settling down to writing a book which he endearingly entitled his *Crudities*. It proved to be one of the most entertaining travel books ever written.

This may well be another.

John Julius Norwich

WARRING ARD PREFAEE TO PREFACE

As no doubt you're well aware, in the world of books a large proportion of readers never bother with prefaces, anxious as they are to get on with the story. With this book, don't skip it as you'll find later on that you don't quite know what's going on and you'll have missed some good bits too. So worried was I about this that I nearly made this Chapter I, but I'm trusting you instead.

Oh, I nearly forgot, we've also put 'gatefolds' in this book, to show off the larger etchings, at enormous expense apparently, so be sure not to miss them either; watch out for this sign.

PREFACE

**F**ollowing the qualified triumphs of my previous work, Graham Clarke's *History of England* (available in some really good bookshops), my publishers handed me a cheque for £4.28, a school exercise book and a brand new HB pencil. *'What's next then lad?'*, they said.

'I thought I'd fulfill a lifetime's ambition and do an illustrated dictionary of North Essex Double Glazing Salesmen 1965–80', says I, 'or maybe a Grand Tour.'

'Excellent idea,' says Phaidon. 'Perfect for us. You could do lots of cutaway drawings and cross sections of door handles, window catches and so on, absolutely fascinating.'

'I was joking about the double glazing idea', says I. 'It was in the nature of a jest.'

'That's the trouble with you Clarke, no one knows whether to take you seriously. It won't do you no good you know.'

'Well I take myself seriously', says I. 'I'm taking myself seriously on a Grand Tour.'

'Right, be off with you then and don't you darken our doors till it's finished, and write a bit neater this time for pity's sake.'

When you consider that Phaidon Press are the absolute tops in the publishing world (at least that's what they told me), it's a wonder that anyone writes books at all nowadays.

Fish Merchant of Venice. 1989. Hand coloured etching, 34.5 × 27.3 cm (13½ × 10¾ in)

THE ARGUMENT

s every schoolboy knows, being English is an honour and a privilege. Who wants Napoleon and stewed frog, when you've already got Biggles and Fish and Chips?

Why anyone should want to go to foreign countries abroad used to be a mystery to me. It was here after all that everything happened. No wonder, for if you draw a straight line from the North Pole to the South Pole and one from somewhere in the West, say New York, to Moscow in the east they cross here in the middle of Kent. Likewise a wobbly line from Stonehenge to Mecca will exactly coincide (see map 1). Anyone not fortunate enough to be born in England it strikes me, should generally be pitied, ridiculed or at least sent food parcels.

Kent was a kingdom long before England which we annexed in about AD 800, and later likewise Scotland, Wales and bits of Ireland, the whole being known universally as GREAT BRITAIN. We don't get this claim even from france ie: Great france is not common parlance.

About two hundred and fifty years ago, the idea struck some intelligent person of the aristocracy* that if he could only pack his wayward son off to the Continent for a spell, it would give the local fox and wench population, and to an extent his bank-balance, a chance to recover. The only way he could get the lad's mother to agree was to pretend it would be a sort of cultural jaunt, and 'round orff the young bounder's education what!' So the Grand Tour was born, and it soon became quite 'the thing'. If there'd been a half decent war going at the time it would have been superfluous, but there wasn't, so the Grand Tour was used instead to temporarily rid the countryside of these noble young gents.

Fashion was everything, and it must have cost 'em a pretty penny to rig 'em out before packing 'em orff. Often it became the ill-deserved lot of some poor servant to accompany the young hero to help get him out of trouble. This luckless article was often referred to as the 'tutor', thereby giving a semi-educational ring to the whole affair, and justifying it for tax purposes. Above all it was a fortunate man who happened to own a travel agents in 1735.

The Grand Tour has taken many diverse forms since then as we shall discover within the pages here presented.

---

* None too common in those days.

INTRO

For those wishing to travel to the foreign parts mentioned herein, this work may well prove a useful guide when planning their own itinerary. And for those who have no such intention (and with whom I am not entirely unsympathetic), with this work to hand they can appear as knowledgeable as the most highly seasoned of travellers, and save a great deal of cash into the bargain.

This volume could be secreted about one's person prior to the dinner party and referred to during visits to the toilet.

"'tis a far better thing that a man appeareth to have a weak bladder than a feeble brain."

W. Shakespeare

It will come as something of a relief to many of my readers to know that since this book is for their enjoyment, and they may have even paid good money for it, there will be absolutely no reference (apart from this) to the subject of Opera. Likewise, references to ballet, french children's table manners, campsite ablutions and scrofulous diseases of the goat will be kept to the very minimum. Those of nervous disposition will find no references to Value Added Tax.

Other persons not mentioned (apart from here) are Stendhal, Proust (Sprout Anag.), Mussolini, J.P. Sartre, Le Corbusier, and Jean Cocteau.

The world of gastronomy, however, is dealt with in some detail, being of particular interest to the present writer, and in this context it would have been irresponsible not to include the requisite accompanying beverages of an intoxicating nature.

No cultural work of this kind would be complete without a section concerning continental lavatorial systems and it has a chapter of its own, perforated for easy removal in case of emergencies.*

My sincere thanks to the art historian and critic, Sir Philip (Phil) Istine, who generously allowed me to make use of his fine library at Wartsand Hall here in Kent. Indeed it was here where I first encountered the Journal of One Tobias Gerkinge Esq. which in many ways was to provide the inspiration for my own travels. Out of gratitude to Sir Philip (and because he probably slipped Phaidon Press a small backhander) we also include some of his own inimitable poetic works. Thanks also to the diaries of that intrepid Victorian traveller and watercolourist, Lady Tankerton-Foxtonsil; and to the Rev. Judas P. Tidmarsh M.A. (racing correspondent of the *Church Times*), whose book *Eye Tiddly Eye Tie* remains a standard work on the subject of Italian wines.

I am sincerely grateful to the writer of the foreword of my book. I had originally hoped to persuade James Julian Ipswich to do the job but am more than happy with the excellent gentleman we were obliged to settle for; it takes courage to do things like that.

* De-Luxe edition only.

Home Sweet Home. 1989. Hand coloured etching, 26.2 × 25 cm (10⅓ × 9⅘ in)

A Green & Pleasant Englishman

'**G**ood amorning, Sir', said the ancient Trussock opening the enormous front door of Wartsand Hall. 'Sir Philip is hexpecting you. Be so magniloquent as to walk this way.' He tottered bowlegged in the direction of the breakfast room. I followed along the gloomy corridor. 'Sir Philip,' he gasped, 'it's Mr er....'.

'More kippers', bellowed the great man, 'and put him in the Library.'

As the kippers were being served, I caught a brief glimpse of Sir Philip in a violet Harris Tweed dressing-gown at his breakfast, using a large Buff-Orpington hen as a table napkin and cooling his cocoa with a cycle pump. 'Be so good as to henter the Library, Sir', said Trussock. 'His knightship will not detain you hay moment.' And he shuffled away to his rat-catching memorabilia, and Dolly Parton record sleeves.

The Library at Wartsand Hall is vast; once the ballroom, it now houses Sir Philip's books, a collection to rival the British Museum, Oxford's Bodleian, or the Victoria and Albert. In fact it may be considered that should he continue to pilfer from these and other institutions at the present rate, one day he will have the greatest collection in the land.

It mattered little that he forgot my presence for nearly six hours. The time was well spent browsing happily among the shelves of splendid volumes and it was here, standing proudly between two large krautenwerken (*Gutenberg's Bible* and *The Nuremberg Chronicles*), that I discovered the book that was to inspire the entire Grand Tour project you hold in your hand. It's spine was of rich green leather, and upon it in large gold lettering were the words:

Ye Astounding and Remarkable Adventures of One Tobias Gerkinge (Gent of Kent.)

I remember the thrill to this day.

Ye Astoundinge & Remarkable Adventures of One Tobias Gorkinge (Gent of Kent)

Hys Journal

Commenced in ye month of Maye in ye yeare of oure Lord 1689 and completed in........

In which this worthy Person lefte hys Native Land in the Kingdon of Kente On England, and journeyed forthe to investigate ye manners, customs, sundry querkes and foybles of distante lands, namely france and Italie.

Mye remarkable journal beginneth: It being ye tenth daye of Maye in the year of our Lord sixteen hundred and eightie nyne.
Being of sound mind and ample body, and having stopped ye milk, I am soon to commence what I am pleased to refer to henceforth as Mye Grande Toure.
I am the first person to use thysse expression for such a journey and it will be another fourtye yearse or so before every Sir Thomas, Lord Richard or Rt.Hon.Harold do it, and nigh on a hundred before every Tom, Dick and Harry venture via Thos. Cook upon such as this; just you wait and see.

My first task was to purchase a sturdy horse suited to mye task, ie: to transport (in addition to my good self), four sides of bacon, a small printing press, sundry potions, powders, tinctures, and requisites and some 'ballast' in the form of firkins of Ale to ye places afformentionede.
To this end I approached one Master G.G. Dobbinger, second-hand horse-salesman and purveyor of equine spare parts:
'This horse, without doubt Sir, is the finest animal in the Kingdom, and for your purpose, good Sir, of pursuing stately progress from one Alehouse to another is utter perfection personified, for he has been pulling the dray for Bladderwraks Brewery for nigh on 40 years; like as not he will render your maps and charts totally superfloo...watsit. Fifty guineas to you Guv and cheap at half the price seein' as you're practically gentry an' all.'
And so it was that the noble beast Tantermount and I became inseparable wayfaring companions.

YE PRAYER, of REV. SEPTIMUS QUIGLEY uttered upon the departure of his friend TOBIAS GERKINGE* ESQ: UPON his GRAND TOURE of 1688

Rev. Septimus Quigley

"O Lord Bless thou our neighbour here, departing upon his brave and wondrous journey. O Lord let not his utterly ridiculous garb and portly stature attract too much mirth from ye blessed natives. Let not Evil befall him we pray, But when it does let not the delightful Miss Lucretia Bumpstead, most charming daughter of two of the finest personages in ye entire County grieve for longer than is respectable (for the man is twice her age y he is a day) Let her choose in his stead a good man O Lord, even a Man of the Cloth. Amen."

Having travelled less than a quarter of a mile in the first hour, I was beginning to feel a distinct lack of nourishments and victuals. But unwilling just yet to begin consuming my own provisions I rested me awhile at ye 'Cat Poacher's Arms', and partook of Luncheon, and a little Port etc. Wisely decided not to venture further that day. Seemed unfortunate though that Eli Gooner and the menne should also attend that evening, but perhaps they had been banished from 'Ye Albion' following ye midday revelling upon my departure. Luckily they attended Ye Bar Publick and I was safely in Ye Saloon, so was not subjected to possible ridicule by those ignorante dolts. It is a well known fact that ye beddes at ye 'Cat Poachers Arms' are not of ye most savorie kind being regularly slept in by many a rapscallion, knave and local estate agente, so I quietly walked home the few hundred yards and had a good night's sleep in my own sensible bedde. Dreamed of the far off landes which I was soon to explore.

CUT HERE
& Place 2 Pieces
172 Yds. 5 ins.
Apart.
For increased
Reality

Please avoid
ships, fish Etc.

NONE GENUINE
WITHOUT THIS
SIGNATURE

DOVER PACKET
...AMSHIP CO.

"...F ALBION RECEDE"

KEY
A.	Proper Castle (part of)
B.	Nice White Cliffs
C.	Decent Pub
D.	Fish & Chip Shops
E.	Green & Pleasant Land
F.	Jolly old Fishermen
G.	Etc.
H.	Etc.

Dedicated to A.W.M.Clarke Esq.
grandfather of the artist who
loved ships.

G.C.G.T. oct/nov.87

"THE SHORES

Bon Chance. 1987. Hand coloured etching, 42.7 × 54.1 cm (16⅘ × 21⅕ in)

11.30 am. Up early. Luckily it was a misty start to the day, and I stealthily made my way back to ye Inne and my faithful horse, Tantermount. He was not a pretty sight for the fool of an ostler had neglected to unload ye saddlebags, trunks and boxes etc. for the night. I swear the beast's legges were full threee inches shorter than when I purchased him for all those precious golden guineas.

Having settled my account with ye Innkeeper and given the ostler a severe buffet in the area where some of us have brains, we set off at about noon eastward towards Dover, the Channel, Paris, Rome....

Passing Mother Trotter's Pie Shoppe on the boundary between our parishes of Crankle Bumpstead* and neighbouring Bog-Twerton is not an easy thing to do at ye beste of tymes as any man do know, but today at half past noon and lunch already an hour overdue, it proved impossible; in any case it may have been months before I tasted their like again. Fine food there mighte possibly be in your french Paris, but not the like of good Mother Trotter's I'll wager. Being yet several hundred yards from ye 'Newt and Dumplings', I was obliged to wash down the dozen or so venison and apricot pies with supplies of my own ale. Would that I had taken it equally from both sides, for Tantermount walked lop-sided as soon as we set off. So, in fairness to the steed, I was obliged to lighten the other barrels; all appeared to have 'travelled welle' as is said, I believe, in the brewing trade. This additional liquid repast somewhat dimmed my expectations of travelling too well myself, however, and a short rest beneath the parish boundary yew trees was considered both wise and welcome.

I did not sleep but when I awoke an hour or so later, the wisdom of my action was somewhat diminished for Tantermount had quite disappeared, and in his place stood a group of urchins, the vileness of which I find it impossible to express with my quill. I might have given several of the little knaves an educational clout, but this proved impossible with my boots buckled together, the discovery of which I made just too late to prevent my pitching headlong in to the adjacent horse trough. Mother Trotter is a kindly enough soul, and my donation of several sovereigns enabled her to gain sufficient strength to pull me out and to persuade her son, little Genghis, to fetch Tantermount from the neighbouring field. A further financial arrangement was entered into with Squire Smeeton's honest baliff over the exact value of the two acres of prime broccoli, which the beast had devoured and which a short while later was to have such a devastating effect on Tantermount's digestive motions.

By this time, it was towards four and thirty after noone, I sensibly banished from my mind all notions of reaching Dover by the forthcoming nightfall, for it was all of fifty long miles. Far more sensible to stable Tantermount and my luggery at ye 'Newt and Dumplings' for the night and set off very early the next morning.

The disgraceful affair at the said alehouse that evening is best left from

* Note: Crankle Bumpstead is the ancient name for Boughton Monchelsea.

these pages, and anyway who would take the word of a half-witted trollop of a Bog-Twerton barmaid to that of the Vice-President of the Crankle Bumpstead League of Sobriety, Fine Scholar, Gentleman (not to say nigh on Aristocrat) and personal friend to the Rev. Septimus Quigley.

It was indeed unfortunate that the maiden concerned should turn out to be Squire Smeeton's daughter Chastity, on holiday from the Convent. The Landlord was gracious enough to suggest I donate twenty guineas towards the dear creature's education, rather than risk a scandal.

The stable lad said Tantermount was almost fully recovered which I took as a tribute to my being an excellent judge of horseflesh. But then with the rudeness one has regretfully learned to expect from such a class of person, he suggested that I was grossly overloading the 'poor beast', especially if I was intending to sit on top of that great pile myself. The pitchfork missed his doltish personage by a whisker, I regret to say.

Rather than waste time stopping as I had done the previous day, I luncheoned on the hoof as it were, enjoying various hams, cheeses, pies and sundry provisions, taking care to keep the 'ship' in trim by drinking a carefully measured five quarts from each of the barrels in turn.

Tantermount maintained his characteristic gait and his special class of stumbling shamble, with his baleful black eye glaring round at me everytime I had to resort to verbal or physical encouragement to ensure our continued progress. However, halfway through the afternoon, he stopped altogether and no amount of encouragement would shift the odiferous quadruped. I noticed that our way lay between two great fields, each supporting a fine crop of broccoli.

I was much gratified that this wretched beast, so low of nature, had learned whilst in my company the inadvisability of gluttony. With my cloak then wrapped around his head as a blindfold, Tantermount proceeded at a speed hitherto unknown. Taking advantage of this, I kindly allowed the garment to remain about the creature's head long after the obnoxious crops had been left behind. And thus we covered a full two miles in but a single hour bringing us to the insignificant hamlet of Lower Twerton wherein I had the choice of ye 'Ratskinners Arms' or the 'Ten Jolly Gravediggers', both famed far and wide for the utterly miserable nature of their landlords, exorbitant prices for ale, cockroaches and poisonous characteristics of victuals supplied by the two most vile-tempered crones in the whole of mid-Kent.

I decided to toss a coin as the best means of choosing which establishment I might grace with my esteemed custom. The Landlords' eyes glinted with avarice and the expectation of lightening the purse of such a fine gentleman; for they must have surely noticed my ease of manner, fine style of dress and handsome steed as they slouched in the doorways of their respective grimy hostelries. My golden guinea glinted in the late afternoon sunlight as I tossed it skyward, and had not the landlord of ye 'Ratskinners Arms' belched, I might well have caught it, but as luck

21

Bon Apetit. 1988. Hand coloured etching, 13.5 × 17.4 cm (5⅓ × 6⅘ in)

would have it, it dropped to the ground where it lodged itself neatly and inextricably between two great paving stones.

Since the coin was quite vertical fate had settled the matter; neither of the ruffians would have my custom that night and with all the dignity in the world and using the head of the offending landlord (who by now was in a crouching posture attempting to retrieve my coin with his corkscrew) as a mounting block, I rode 'swiftly' away.

All that now stood between Tantermount, my good self and ye 'Haddocks Arms' at Twerton St. Mildred – yet a full six dark miles distant – were acres of bleak farmland in the midst of which lay the massive structure of a castle surrounded by a moat of foul water, home of the legendary man-eating pike, Black Sydney.

At the thought of this, but for my natural valour, I might well have turned back. However a gentleman must behave as a gentleman for 'nothing behoves a pumpkin insomuch as a scoffing turkeycock', as my old mother so frequently said.

So I felt obliged to turn right at Hangman's Cross and crave a night's lodging at the ancestral home of Baron Philtheriche de Philtheriche of Gawdsakes Castle. Though not famous for hospitality, surely they would not turn away a personage such as I, scholar etc., etc., so far from home and hearth. However, some unknown fear seemed to beset Tantermount for he began dreadful shivering as we approached the gaunt gatehouse towers, black against a blacker sky. And though it was a chill night my compassionate nature compelled me to wrap my cloak about his head for the comfort of his weak spirit. At this we sped forward and had the drawbridge actually been lowered we might well have gained a warm night's lodging in fine style; as it was the waters of the moat seemed uncommonly cold for late May......

The unfortunate Gerkinge must have survived his 'early bath' in order to record it for us in his journal, but alas it is the final entry; the remaining 3,804 or so pages being entirely blank, but for some water staining and what appear to be the tooth marks of a large fish. The waters of Leeds Castle moat (for research reveals that Gerkinge's Gawdsakes Castle was indeed the earlier name of our famed Leeds Castle) had not only dampened his body, but it seems his spirits too, and it is likely that he returned home a damper but wiser man. We sincerely trust that his reverend colleague had not found time to marry the delightful Lucretia during the two days of his absence.

Though Gerkinge's travels must be considered something of a failure, I found in them the inspiration for my own adventures as recorded herein, which same I undertook by way of a small tribute to his pioneering spirit. And though I travelled a great deal further, it is curious to relate that I too met a fate not unlike that of poor Gerkinge; but more of that later.

Black Sydney
(205 lbs.)

23

MY OLD MAN SAID FOLLOW VINCENT VAN AND DONT DILLY WITH DALI ON THE WAY

True they look quite nice (from some angles, side rather than front or back), but I'm afraid the horse was quite quickly rejected as the most convenient method of transport for *my* Grand Tour.

It had to be considered, though, as the horse, with or without some form of carriage fixed to it, would have undoubtedly been the main method of transport enjoyed by my predecessors on their Grand Tours. At a leisurely pace and from on high in the saddle or carriage, the unfolding scene could be fully appreciated. Fresh air and exercise were to be had a-plenty and the whole affair was relatively cheap to run. If the local populace should turn offensive or the dogs be set loose, a quick dig in the ribs would accelerate the whole show out of trouble. On the other hand, horses have a funny look in their eyes, especially it seems when looking at me. Not only that but they are a bit smelly and of course are apt to slew violently sideways without warning.

The solution, a method of transport that seemed to possess most of these advantages and none of the drawbacks, and one which stood in semi-retirement in an old shed in our garden. He was large, black, and had no doubt been considered handsome in his day. With a flat back tyre and a large basket in front, a tradesman's delivery bike was the answer. The breed ridden by skinny-legged, nobbly-kneed youths to convey goods for nigh on a hundred years. The butcher, the baker, and the stripy-aproned grocer all employed their services. Sturdy and cheap to run, some of the lucky little lads riding them could earn as much as tuppence-farthing a month I'm told. And, if not killed by tram or mad cart-horse, any lad worth his salt might well look forward to being an assistant on the cheese counter by the time he was fifty or sixty.

My own specimen of the breed had much of the strength and weight of a cart-horse, a vital attribute for I intended to carry much luggage in the great wicker basket up front, and perhaps bring a trailer up behind. Perhaps even a caravan! Yes, a caravan, small and cosy; the gypsies had the right idea, this was the way to see Europe without doubt. In due course and with the kind assistance of Kevin 'You draw it I can make it' Martin of Mereworth, it became a reality.

Readers of this work who hitherto have acquainted themselves with the geography of the france and Italy areas from the closing pages of their 1956 Boy's Own Diary will know france to be an unsightly green splurge between (beige) Luxembourg and (orange) Spain, while Italy is the (yellow) boot dangling out of the bottom of Europe attempting to kick poor little Sicily (the Italian Isle of Wight) into the Atlantic.

One cannot recommend too highly the use of proper maps for those planning to travel in foreign parts; the Boy's Own Diary offerings are just not detailed enough for the purpose one finds. Beware of later maps that get the colours wrong too; you'll see all kinds of places coloured British Empire pink nowadays, when they have no right whatsoever to this honour. If we'd wanted them to be pink, we'd have been good enough to colonize them.

Neither my editor nor I wished to include the following piece for obvious reasons. However, Sir Philip is a man of some influence in the world of Art Publishing so common sense prevailed.

While mooching round in Thomas Cooks
I nicked one of them travel books;
Here's a cheaper holiday –
Europe on ten quid a day,
With slight adjustment for inflation.
Got tickets at Victoria Station;
A final taste of English grub,
Took two days cash in the Railway Pub;
My first rail trip was now begun
So started reading chapter one.
A B.R. pie, though high in price,
Contained ingredients 'not quite nice';
And with no paper on the train,
Chapter two went down the drain.

Sir P. Istine

Speed on down to famous Dover,
Our English Channel to cross over;
Seek not dark and doubtful tunnel,
Choose something floating with a funnel.
While sailors up on duty freeze,
You lounge about and take your ease,
Dreaming of your duty-frees.

I must admit when seas get rough,
I really am not quite so tough;
Too much up and down will spoil it,
with frequent visits to the toilet;
At least the bar is always handy
To get yourself a port and brandy.

But today it's calm and sunny,
So join the queue, and change your money;
Don't these froggy notes look funny?
They look so odd to you and me,
'Cos they've got no Royalty ... you see.
Wave to England, your last chance,
Before you know it, you're in france;
Suddenly the crowd goes frantic,
And swarms ashore this land Romantic.

Will customs men in little sheds
Look dubious and shake their heads?
Will our passports in this state
Suddenly be out of date?
Will the gendarmes bash our cars?
Will there be bitter in the bars?

Pluck up courage fearful lad,
Many frenchmen aren't too bad;
And if you smile and say 'Bonjour',
You'll quite enjoy your first Grand Tour.
Fear not the garlic, nor the frog,
Fear not the snail, or wine and grog;
Avoid french drivers in the fog,
And travellers – beware the bog!

Standing up or sitting down,
'Facilities' will make you frown;
(a little chap might even drown).
So famous for their french cuisine,
They're not so good at 'la latrine';
Tops at art and wine and trains,
They're the pits when it comes to drains.

Carte Antico. 1989. Hand coloured etching. 13.6 × 17.2 cm (5⅓ × 6⅘ in)

OPERATION JOHNNY GARLIC SAUSAGE

Aany of the world's pink bits, our former colonies, and parts of Empire etc., had the good sense long after they'd sent us home to hang on to cricket. Places like India, New Zealand, West Indies and even Australia were sensible enough to know a good thing when they saw it. Not so your United States of America however, and this unfortunate failure stands as an utterly uncrossable rift between our respective cultures. One assumes that they consider Hamlet to be a reasonable drama and that Elgar knew how to turn out a decent symphony. Let them take our word for it then that cricket is yet another sublime achievement of humanity's endeavour on this earth and that their lives are less wonderful without it.*

I just thought I'd mention it, no offence.

BIOGRAPHICAL NOTE
concerning

Captain Percival Hector Maximillian Jonah Gasbiscuit
O.B.E.

Only son of Sir Basil Barton-Chumpstead Gasbiscuit and Lady Verity, formerly head-girl of Fangleton Court Reform School.

'Captain' was of course his first name not his military rank; despite his soldierly bearing and neat appearance he was in fact declared unfit for national service (by his mother) in 1914. The O.B.E. signifies 'Opening Bat Extraordinary', an honour which he bestowed upon himself at the age of ten.

* N.B. Dear editor, should we delete this bit from the U.S. edition? G.

Yours Truly's Bally Cricket Mission 1922
Capt. Percy Gasbiscuit O.B.E.

After the bally scrummage of your Great War it was pretty obvious to a chap that the whole shooting match would have reached close of play a bally sight sooner had the Johnny Foreigners of this world been equipped with the slightest notion of how to play the magnificent game of cricket. Four days is absolute maximum when it comes to a cricket match, but your bally Continentals made the Great War last four years – bally appalling show.

Courage, fair play, team spirit, and a sense of when enough is enough are qualities seriously lacking in certain quarters, and so the idea came to me to mount an expedition of some sort to put things in order, i.e.: teach your actual french etc. how to play 'The Game'.

My old chum Gervase Swaffleton-Croake and I picked our team pretty carefully as you can imagine. No room in this particular jaunt for bally duffers or bad-eggs etc. Mustn't let the side down in front of Johnny Foreigner. What!?

Luckily, Piers Drone-Gawkley's old man was the proprietor of (amongst nearly everything else in the area) the Mid-Kent General Omnibus Co., so the selection of good old Piers, though bally awful at cricket, was vital to ensure the provisions of the required motor charabanc and driver. The latter turned out to be one Jones (Albert, Mr) who was persuaded to act also as travelling groundsman, baggage master, purser, butler, valet, laundry maid, matron and twelfth man; straight as a die and no wish to better himself.

After a certain amount of flim flam, shilly-shally and general indecisiveness amongst my chums in the Upper Biffington Cricket Club, the eventual team list ran thus:

1. Capt. Percy Gasbiscuit O.B.E. (Captain) (Ones good self)
2. Hon. Jasper Bamforth G.B.H.
3. Rev. 'Ernest' Skellington-Coote (Chaplain)
4. Denzil Strewth
5. Gervase Swaffleton-Croake (Vice)
6. Timothy Pearson-Newt
7. Hon. Lucian Beamish-Smeeth (Ukelele)
8. K. 'Tosher' Holroyd
9. Piers Drone-Gawkley
10. Professor Quentin Beazley-Skink (Fossils, Etc.)
11. The Man McTavish

Plus Jones, Albert, Mr (Chara etc., etc.)

Rue de Wakening. 1988. Hand coloured etching. 54 × 69.1 cm (21⅕ × 27⅕ in)

To be honest, a couple of the chaps were not previously known to me: the professor, apparently an erstwhile colleague of Denzil Strewth's old man in turf Accountancy; and the man McTavish, a person of the Scottish persuasion who apparently got chatting to Hon. Lucian Beamish-Smeeth at his ukelele classes. For some reason McTavish was anxious to distance himself from possible eye-contact with members of the Constabulary, and was only too keen to make up the numbers at the last minute. It was only when we had actually crossed the bally English Channel that the bounder revealed that he had never played cricket in his entire life; comes from being a bally Johnny Bagpipes no doubt, and in any case he intended leaving us as soon as we got anywhere near Paris; a thoroughly rotten Scotch egg.

Thus it was that we were obliged to enlist the services of Jones, Albert, Mr as a playing member of the team and a damn fine wicket-keeper he proved to be too, even though he did insist on using his bus driver's gloves for the purpose. I decided to overlook this minor eccentricity, as did not consider it a detail your french person was likely to object to.

A day or two before departure we were oiling our bats, etc., and generally spivving up our togs, when old Tosher Holroyd has the most brilliant idea. 'Why not take our bally cricket pavilion along with us, so we could brace ourselves with a bally snifter now and then? Can't trust the bally french to have too many decent bally cricket pavilions about, what!'

Jones, Albert, Mr informs us that our own building would prove a bit weighty from a towing point of view, but nearby Hoppington St. Fergus C.C. has a most suitable example and should we decide to borrow it he could oblige with some wheels, etc. No time to negotiate terms actually, so 'borrowed' pavilion during hours of darkness, i.e. at night. Lot of bally duffers over in Hoppington anyway, we've beaten them for the last six years on the trot. 'Regard it as Hoppington C.C.'s contribution to International understanding etc.', says Rev. 'Ernest' Skellington-Coote; damn clever chap actually, got exams and everything – a devastating spin bowler and drinks like a bally haddock. Sort of cove that could get your Johnny dog-collar a good name actually.

Luckily the pavilion shelves are pretty well stocked already, but took the precaution of adding a few dozen cases of claret from Swaffleton-Croakes' old man's cellars, supplemented by champagne no longer required for Drone-Gawkley's peoples' Wedding Anniversary (as his old man has gone off with the new parlourmaid). Bally handy for us as you can hardly expect the french to have any decent champagne about the place.

Come early June, preparations appeared to be complete. The pavilion was hitched on and after a certain amount of general tearfulness from the mothers, fiancées, nannies, aunts, sisters, womenfolk etc, we set off in fine style, flags flying, engine roaring and ukelele at full strum; bally card our Hon. Lucian Beamish-Smeeth, I can tell you.

The journey to Dover was remarkable only for the number of times our

Pearson-Newt required the 'comfort of bushes' and the rest of the team celebrated its forthcoming triumphant tour by swigging the odd glass. Quite how the eleven of us got through eight dozen bottles of champagne in a journey of but forty or so miles is a mystery to me, but then mathematics etc. was never my best subject, as anyone at St. Judas's will no doubt be delighted to inform you.

Bally Channel crossing a bit much, not only for Pearson-Newt, but most of the others too including yours truly, I'm obliged to say. Denzil Strewth says he reckons the champagne must have been 'a bit off'. Drone-Gawkley, jolly upset, says we didn't ask Strewth's opinion regarding the quality of his old man's champagne, and considers chucking Strewth's cricket cap over the bally side of the bally boat – with Strewth's head still inside it.

The calming influence of Jones, Albert, Mr is brought to bear and before you know it we're landing in bally Calais, france, land of snails' legs etc., etc., and we don't know what including garlic etc.

Jones, Albert, Mr soon shows he is pretty nifty at driving on wrong side of road as he got some experience in the bally fourteen-eighteen do apparently, and we're soon rattling through france like a bat out of hell. Pearson-Newt now travelling in the pavilion at his own convenience as it were, but remainder of team in high spirits.

Most of the chaps had never crossed the bally Channel before, so bally good laugh all round at oddities of french carryings on in general, and bally stupid flat hats in particular; ukelele at full throttle, absolute card Beamish-Smeeth, mother was 'on the stage' etc. General idea is to stop in centre of selected town or village and generally persuade locals etc. to pick a side from amongst the most sporting chaps around and generally thrash the living daylights out of them in a one day friendly, thus by example generally educating the blighters. Our professor can apparently speak actual french which should make negotiations even simpler.

Eventually call a halt in a likely looking place called Something St. bally french Ville or other, about half way to Paris. Locals absolutely fascinated by chara and pavilion etc., but don't appear to grasp general idea of things, i.e. to play cricket match for educational purposes.

Professor reckons they think we are bally travelling theatre company! Utter sauce! However Beamish-Smeeth seizes God-given opportunity and does some impromptu ukelele numbers from pavilion steps. Had he more than three pieces in his repertoire I feel he might well have gone on all day. As it was his short performance was well received by the bally locals who promptly encouraged one of their own number to fetch his bally accordion from his café. It's a well known fact that if there's one thing that is guaranteed to get on a chap's nerves, it's the bally squeeze-box. So I exercised my authority and ordered a speedy but dignified retreat, much against the wishes of bally ukelele Smeeth and the man McTavish who had got into 'conversation' with some young women – they did not look

Johnny Garlic Sausage. 1989. Hand coloured etching, 34.1 × 54.4 cm (13½ × 21½ in)

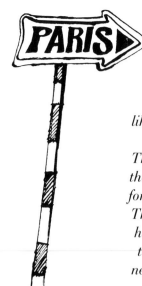

like the sort of nuns we are accustomed to back home, whatever he might say.

The less said about the roadside lodging house selected for our first night the better. Pearson-Newt reckoned his mother would have 'had a fit', and for once in the tour he gained our complete sympathy and understanding. The professor alone was delighted with affairs as he was fairly certain he had discovered at least six new varieties of bed bug previously unknown to science. The final blow was dealt when we were informed there were neither grilled kippers nor devilled kidneys for breakfast, reducing two or three of my men to tears; bally bad show.

Once more on the road we celebrated with a case of Swaffleton-Croake's old man's thirty-five-year-old Chateau Whatsit.

Pearson-Newt bitten by dog, Strewth kindly provides fascinating lecture on Rabies.

So far have been quite unable to spot flat piece of grass large enough to swing a bally cat, let alone play cricket. This does not bode well. Village after bally village utterly lacking in this respect, serious knock to morale of team in general and my good self in particular. Denzil bally Strewth says he's not a bit surprised as it's common knowledge the french don't have grass! A bit bally strong, what? A chap can only take so much.

All feel much revived after rather decent lunch in 'La Petite Restaurant Angleterre', whatever that might mean. Foreign food it may be but bally edible all the same. But whole applecart completely upset when Denzil Strewth tells our Timothy Pearson-Newt he's just eaten frogs' legs. Newt takes on some of the colouring and facial characteristics of the said amphibian, and we usher him towards the pavilion again to discover the man McTavish replacing the contents of several cricket bags with a wide selection of our best vintage supplies prior to his planned Parisian disembarkation. Whether he ever escaped from the vileness of the adjacent stone cow sheds is a matter for conjecture. One cares not. Good riddance to the blighter say I.

While arranging this jaunt 'Operation Johnny Garlic Sausage', as we called it, my old man pretty well insisted that we don't spend too much time in bally Paris as it's not the sort of set up apparently that a chap ought to get to know too well. My old man's word is good enough for me, but not for Denzil bally clever devil Strewth apparently; his old man reckons a few days in Paris is part of a chap's education, and if a chap's come all the way to bally france, it's a bit bally stupid if a chap can't spend a few days in bally Paris if a chap wants.

However, Jones wisely skirts right around bally Paris and before long, and to our universal joy, we spot an absolutely top rate piece of turf, the front lawn of a bally great house at some place called Versailles. Actually bigger than Biffington Hall and Hoppington Grange put together; this chap's folks must have an absolute bally packet, etc. Bashed in stumps for the first time......

My chums and I who play a little cricket
Travelled south to seek a 'nouveau wicket';
Hoping that there might be just a chance
To introduce our noble game to france.
With bats and caps and trousers of white flannel
We found a boat and crossed the choppy channel.
If we could find a decent bit of grass
Our chances might be reckoned as first class;
Looking round about we said, 'Aye, Aye!
There's a notice over there that says Versailles.'
A nice front lawn entirely without bumps –
So we picked our team and walloped in the stumps.

I'm sure some readers will be wondering just having read this remarkable account of such an important event in cricketing history, why more has not been heard of this expedition. I too was fascinated and made enquiries in the appropriate quarters. I eventually tracked down Jones, Albert, Mr, who though nearly one hundred years old, still has his wits about him. His answer ran thus:

'Well young Sir, we did heventually find a village down in your france area what managed to rustle hup some sort of a team. Has I recalls, it consisted of four nuns, an old bloke with a gammy leg, a load of scruffy little boys and a blind dog. They beat us by an innings and eighty-six runs, so we come 'ome'.

A rather sad conclusion, I think you would agree, to a noble and idealistic endeavour, but maybe one which was doomed to failure anyway. Perhaps Captain Percy and his fellows may have had more of a civilizing influence than they realized, for you can still see old men practising underarm bowling all over france – even if they still haven't got a decent bit of turf to do it on.

GASTRONOTE

If you're going to feel sorry for anyone having to eat frogs legs, feel sorry for the frog.

From the eater's point of view they are quite tasty, a sort of mini chicken leg (not at all green and warty); in fact, they taste very un-frog like.

This is not true of snails which do taste snail-like, but are usually so doused in garlic and what-not you can't be too certain about it.

Like so many overpriced 'gourmet' dishes, they sprang from the starving peasants' hunger and ingenuity, rather than from your so-called master chef's expertise. Snails must be easier to catch than frogs of course. Did you know all snails are called Maurice?

ROUEN

Rouen is a very friendly city and if this book had been but just one page thicker I'd definitely have done an etching of the fine cathedral. It's here that the English are said to have burnt Joan of Arc. It's not something one likes to be reminded of. My own answer to this accusation was that it happened not all that many centuries after the infamous Norman Conquest of England (Normans were really Vikings but for our present purpose we must pretend they were frenchmen); and Normans were still 'in charge of things' as it were, especially when it came to making up rules about who could execute who (or whom even). So the french actually burnt the poor girl themselves. Ha! Ha!

'Now look 'ere Miss Arc, what's all this about dressing up as a soldier and unnerving the lads?'.
'I wers terld to by Gerd Erlmarty.'
'In English or french, Miss.'
'Whay in frensh erf ceurse.'
'God does not speak french Miss, as you well know. You are to be bruléed immediatement as a common witch, and as the leader of a load of cowardly nurks what make a young lady go in front.'

GASTRONOTE

Fish do especially funny things with their names when they travel to france or Italy, so beware. Don't for goodness' sake expect the waiter to translate a fish name for you, he'll just hold his hands a certain distance apart and wobble one of them; such is his command of English fish nomenclature.

Reine de la Mer. 1988. Hand coloured etching. 34.4 × 27.2 cm (13½ × 10¾ in)

La Tres Chose. 1988. Hand coloured etching, 34.6 × 27.3 cm (13½ × 10¾ in)

GETTING PLASTERED in PARIS & RUE DE WAKENING

Has it not occurred to even the most casual of visitors to the exalted Art Galleries of Paris why there are so few works by artists whose surnames begin with the letter 'A'? 'What about Arp?', I hear someone muttering to himself. His name began with an 'H' (arp is merely slack continental pronunciation); anyway he was hardly heard of at all until he took over his father's lager business.

Be assured you will find not one; plenty of Bonnards, Cezannes and the odd Degas and so on right through the artistic alphabet to Émile and Gordon Zola. But no 'A's.

Herewith the solution to this mystery. It is to be found in chapter 807 of this splendid autobiographical work by Sir Philip (Phil) Istine.

Paris, 19th November 1937

Tried to book in at the rather impressive Hotel de Ville; but once again was refused a room. Retreated to more modest establishment in the 6th Herrison* or Latin Quarter, 'La Belle Poubelle' administered by one Madame Mitzi Duplonk.

I dare say few of my readers have ever heard of the 'Ecole' about to be discussed and it's brilliant but ill-fated director, Vernon Mallard. The shelves of the world's great libraries yield but little concerning this most remarkable of men. The publishers of the finest volumes on the 'History and Development of Art'** have as yet devoted little attention to his extraordinary genius, yet who can blame them?

It was my intention to 'play detective' whilst staying in this city, to unravel once and for all the mystery of this remarkable Englishman who for a brief span held such great influence over Parisian artistic circles in the early part of this century and who, but for his untimely disappearance, would have undoubtedly gone on to become one of the greatest painters of all time. Another Rembrandt, Leonardo, Picasso or Mervyn Cruddy R.A. perhaps?

* We assume he means Arrondissement. Herrison is a hedgehog [Ed.]

** Phaidon Press, Oxford.

RUE FRANÇAISE

It will surprise few of my more intelligent readers to learn that the french would have preferred that this 'mere Englishman' had never visited Paris at all. The mention of his name in artistic circles only serves to bring an even more blank and uncomprehending stare than is usual among such persons.

As a modest dabbler in oils myself I was well acquainted with the several dozen establishments proffering artists' materials in this Latin Quarter, and decided that this would be my most obvious starting point. After all was it not in this very area that I had first discovered that fading plaque above the crumbling portico, reading 'Ecole de Trois Canards Volants' (prop. Vernon Mallard) some years before?

I had called on at least a dozen shops, but alas the assistants were far too young to remember a customer of thirty odd years before, however distinguished. I was about to close my investigations for the day and brace myself with a Gallic snifter in a local hostelry, when I found myself peering through a grimy window cluttered with dusty white Venus de Milos, sickly cupids and severed feet with the name 'Senilier' inscribed sheepishly above it. Amid the gloomy scene within (reminding me of nothing so much as a painting by Honoré Daumier on one of his off days) stood an ancient bent figure. His brown coat reached the floor, and resembled a length of sacking draped over a walking stick, while his head was almost entirely moustache and fruit drop spectacles, the latter drooping over an uncooked baguette of a nose. I took this person to be Monsieur le Patron, and ventured in.

M. Senilier

I speak little Latin myself, having never entertained the notion to become either quack doctor or director of Kew Gardens. Imagine my surprise and delight when he said in croaking but otherwise almost perfect french: 'Mornin' Guvnor, and what might I do for you?'

'I wish to ask you a few questions', I replied. 'Tell me good sir, did you perchance have doings with any of the major artistic figures of the early twentieth Century?'

'Certainly did Guv', he said, pouring himself a large Beaujolais from a bottle concealed amongst the red inks. 'Knew 'em all I did. Manet, Monet, Minet, Munet, Auguste Renoir and his brother Septembre, Edvard and Thelonius Munch, Maindrain – sold 'im 'is first junior paint box I did, and a ruler of course. Vincent Van Gogh come 'ere regular 'e did; poor old lad, still owes me six francs. Glass of turps?'

'Thank you' I said, warily taking the proffered waterpot of carmine beverage. 'And tell me, did you know of one Vernon Mallard, director of the Ecole de Trois.....'

'Vernon? Know 'im? Why he was my best customer for years. A real gent. Used paint very thick and paid cash. Can't ask for more than that. Shame about 'is terrible end, eh Guv?'

So I had found the man, perhaps the only man in the whole of Paris, who could tell me, what I so needed to know. I called in at his shop many times during the next week or so. He seemed to enjoy our 'chats'; I provided a case or two of cheap wine each day while the old boy provided the following:

Vernon Truform Mallard arrived in Paris by mistake in the summer of 1907, full of ambition, zeal and a burning desire to get away from his native land. His talent had manifested itself some time before when in the Biggleswade Arts and Crafts Autumn Do he had walked away with the Alderman Fitzgibbon's Cup for 'a good effort' in plasticine (over 18s). This comparatively modest achievement, combined with his love of avian natural history (he was a devoted reader of the Rev. Thurston-Crake's column in the Bedfordshire Methodist Wildfowler, every other Thursday, $2\frac{1}{2}$d.) set the seal upon his future. Thus at the tender age of twenty-nine he left home for good and set out for Brisbane.

Through an unfortunate series of mis-managements by travel agents, booking clerks, porters and cab drivers, he arrived in Paris five months later and promptly decided to look no further. For Paris in those days provided everything he sought; agreeably dull, uninspiring and utterly predictable, it was a refreshing contrast to the cosmopolitan, easy-going hurley-burley and fierce artistic vitality of his home town. For him Paris was a 'blank canvas', a barren land merely awaiting his genius to bring it to life.

Perhaps the inspiration for his flying ducks came from his wanderings across native heath as a lad or from the fact that his father was the most notorious poacher and poultry thief in Southern England, who knows. Suffice it to say this remarkable art-form reached its zenith beneath his inspired brush.

Just why the ducks should always fly from left to right with beaks slightly open, why the smallest should be in front with the largest bringing up the rear is an enigma for far more learned scholars even than I. Suffice it to say that the subtleties of alignment, flying angle and positioning within the rectangle were of the utmost importance, nay, were brought to perfection by Mallard. Had he stuck to his own canvases and not started to improve fellow artists' already completed works, he would certainly have avoided trouble.

Whilst his applying Les Trois Canards Volants to every canvas by all the artists whose surname began with 'A'* in the dozen or so major Art Galleries and Museums of Paris represents an enormous personal achievement, it was also the cause of his undoing and eventual disgrace.

* Exceptions were those by Anon. Mallard considered that the works by Anonymous Bosch contained enough wildlife already.

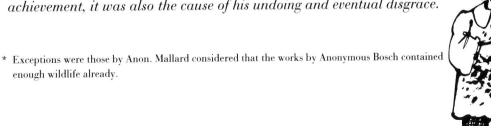

Piece de Resistance. 1988. Hand coloured etching, 54.6 × 69.2 cm (21½ × 27⅕ in)

His method of procedure was apparently thus: he would arrive at his chosen gallery just before dusk and proceed to the Greco-Roman Statue Dept. which was naturally deserted but for the customary dozing attendant. When the closing bell rang this person would depart wearily for 'cloaks' to collect beret and déjèuner box. By the time he had returned to check all was well before going home, Mallard had removed his clothes and was balancing on one leg on his paint box amongst the other statues, where his pallid complexion and strained expression made him indistinguishable from his surroundings. With his palette in one hand as a shield and marl-stick in the other as a rapier, he looked a perfect Horatio, Hercules or Ariadne. Five minutes later he would begin.

In order to achieve a good bond between the original and his own vital additions, Mallard was obliged to roughen the surface giving it a brisk rub-down with medium-grade glass paper. He would then begin painting, and on a good night he could improve twenty or thirty pieces before locking himself in the gents just prior to opening time early the following morning.

Hardly a week or two had gone by when the curators and customers of these grand establishments began to notice certain elaborations carried out on their precious 'works of art'. In a display of classic continental over-reaction the several hundred works were immediately removed and burnt.

There was little doubt, of course, as to who had perpetrated these 'offences' as they were regarded, for with the mastery of touch, subtle colouring and incomparable positioning it could only be the master himself and not merely the work of his faithful apprentices Braque, Chagall and Seurat.

The authorities set a trap and on August 10, 1910 Mallard was apprehended just as he was about to begin work on Mrs. Bonnard getting out of the bath. He could offer no excuse, for around him lay the incriminating tools of his trade, paints, brushes, marl-stick and stuffed ducks. In the excitement of the moment the poor man had forgotten to put on his clothes, and they were later found draped over Aphrodity at the Waterhole, circa 210 B.C.

His trial was a farce even by french standards, undoubtedly made worse by his choosing to conduct his own defence in a Bedfordshire dialect. Inevitably he was given the severest of punishments. There was however a choice: either the guillotine straight, a front row seat at the first night of Benvenuto Strangulati's latest opera, or to spend the rest of his days in the Foreign Legion under the burning skies of the Sahara. For him the choice was plain, and with the utmost dignity he tucked the edge of his red-spotted artist's hanky beneath the rear of his Biggleswade 2nd Eleven's cricket cap and proceeded from the courtroom in a manner intended to portray the motion of a two-seater Bedouin Infantry Camel. Such eloquence reduced even the stern french judiciary to tears.

As a consequence and with uncustomary sensitivity he was granted a last wish and was allowed (under heavily armed guard) to visit for the last time, Materiaux de Beaux Arts chez Senilier. Here, with drooping shoulders and tears in his eyes, he selected a Duke of Windsor and Newton's eight colour 'Bijou' water colour box, a couple of No.3 sable, series A brushes and a small student's grade sketch pad. With no money about his person, Monsieur Senile graciously accepted Van Gogh's 'Sunflowers' which Mallard produced from the poacher's pocket of his father's Derby tweed shooting jacket, and with the aid of some Beaujolais Nouveau cleaned the bloody ducks off the top left-hand corner.

From: 'The Cultural Memoirs' by Sir Philip Istine (Lurking Hyena Press, 1939)

GASTRONOTE

One of the most difficult tasks liable to beset the Grand Tourist is the buying of a corkscrew in Paris. 'Don't be even more stupid than usual Clarke', I hear you say. 'The place must be riddled with them.' So it is, but they all belong to waiters, barmen, restaurateurs etc., who of course would be only too delighted to open a bottle on your behalf should you care to purchase at their prices, but are quite unwilling to lend it for you to open bottles purchased at the corner shop. The corner shops of course can't stock corkscrews or they would get their windows broken by the Guild of Master Bar-stewards. Ironmongers (if you can find such a premises in Paris) won't stock them for similar reasons, except on very pricey Swiss penknives where the corkscrew is hidden away amongst several dozen other blades and is too small to be effective anyway. It's a sad state of affairs and can lead a man into bad habits, i.e. drinking wine that needs no corkscrew, either the cheapest of Supermarket plonks with a little plastic cap; or worse still champagne with its self-exploding cork, fizz-fozz of the nobs.

TRAVEL CHECKLIST

Corkscrew, can-opener, Union Jacks (various sizes), Marmite*, Bovril, proper mustard, sun-helmet, crates brown ale, flea-powders, marmalade, bloater paste, passport, corkscrew, penknife, cribbage board, maps, foreign money, concertina, small printing press*, puncture repair outfit, Teddy, notebooks, drawing materials, yoyo, sunglasses, foreign word dictionary, whoopee cushion; oh yes, digestive disorder correctives (assorted), spare socks and a corkscrew.

*optional

47

MONET IS THE ROOT OF ALL EVIL

In my largely unsuccessful campaign to disprove the iniquitous puritanical theory that 'you can have too much of a good thing', I've taken considerable academic interest in food and drink. Especially on occasions such as the present moment when I find myself in Paris, a city which honours itself with the title of the gastronomic capital of Europe and therefore the entire Universe.

Just where this idea came from is something of a mystery to the thinking man; indeed why should the french 'language' be the standard parlance of the world of food at all? In England it is simply used to keep prices high and portions small as we well know. But the fact remains that the whole world of restaurateurism is riddled with frenchmen both real and simulated; and so we are obliged to have this fact stuffed continuously down our gullets or risk starvation, particularly in Paris.

The following yarn, however, goes some little way to redress this imbalance and put things in perspective. I am assured it is absolutely true for it was originally told to Sir Philip Istine by a man of the church as absolute gospel; in fact, it was none other than the Reverend Judas P. Tidmarsh, V.S.O.P., former racing correspondent of the Church Times. Its veracity is therefore beyond question.

 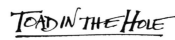 

GASTRONOTE

TOAD IN THE HOLE

Translates rather interestingly as 'Crapaud dans le Trou', but don't expect to find it on the menu. The french have a great deal yet to learn with regard to fine cooking.

UNE CHARGEMENT DE VIEUX CABBILAUD FRAPPEZ
(A Load of Old Cod's Wallop)

LINGUANOTE

Voila. 1988. Hand coloured etching, 13.6 × 17.3 cm (5⅓ × 6⅘ in)

Herewith an extract from his memoirs:

Une Chargement de Vieux Cabbilaud Frappez

Gannet's Guide Gastronomique*, *or the* Gourmet's Bible *as we call it, lists hundreds of restaurants in Paris, but none are more highly acclaimed than the three I am about to mention;* La Bonne Poubelle, Taverne et Grottes Crapaudique *and* Les Boules de Singe Bronzé.

The curious thing is that all three are not only on the same side of the very same street in the very smartest district of the city, but also absolutely adjacent to each other. Each receives in the 'good book' the very highest award possible, i.e. four crossed frying pans and six portefeuilles mort. The resultant rivalry between the three exalted proprietor-chefs is legendary and exceeded only by the mutual hatred of their three extremely beautiful wives. These ladies might frequently be observed quite openly tripping up next door's waiters or pouring hot coffee in each other's ice buckets. At the time in question, I was religious affairs correspondent to the Licensed Victualler *and as such still had an expense account, so I decided to investigate this fascinating phenomenon. By committing a minor falsehood, i.e. letting slip that I was the chief inspector for* Gannet's Guide, *I managed to secure a table for two in each of the establishments on three consecutive nights.*

My companion on each occasion was Miss Thelma Tewkes-fformwork, *the well known exotic dancer and steeplechase jockey, and of course a devout glutton in her own right.*

We were graciously greeted at La Bonne Poubelle *by Madame Za Za Duplonk herself. This establishment as you may know was where Choufleur de Couteaulerie was conceived and reached near perfection. Literally translated as 'the shuffling of cutlery', the tableware (including dishes, plates, wine glasses etc., as well as the knives and forks) might be deftly changed as many as six or seven times during the course of a meal. The corresponding two hundred per cent increase in prices was considered superb value for money by an admiring clientele. To go into details of each course may be considered superfluous to our purposes here, but suffice it to say the Loin of Walrus (cooked pink) with Smoked Apricot and Crocus stuffing delicately baked to golden perfection was probably the best I've ever experienced. Whilst my guest described her Iguana Strogonoff with Wild Lark's Tonsils in Tarragon brandy as 'absolutely scrummy!'*

Eventually the screams, shouts and curses which had sporadically emerged from the direction of the hallowed kitchen, together with the sounds of breaking glass and crashing fish kettles, subsided, and l'homme illustré himself emerged to loud applause from his amply repleted

Thelma
Tewkes-fformwork

* Published annually by Pigglé et Cochonicque

* Hamlet (anag.)

devotees. He was a short sturdy man, round of face with thick pebble glasses and splendid waxed moustache. He spoke not a word, apparently he seldom did, but courteously kissed the hands of the ladies present and one or two of the men as well by mistake; evidently his short sight was real enough. There was something oddly familiar about him, however, that I could not identify. I graciously accepted the gift of a priceless magnum of Cheval Blanc 1947 and his good wishes to the noble publishers of Gannet's Guide.

The next evening we inspected La Taverne et Grottes Crapaudique, quite different in style (although equally expensive of course). It was here that Jean-Luc Chevalviande conceived Cuisine Disparu, and, as we know, during it's zenith portions got so small that they actually disappeared altogether; the beautiful descriptions in the enormous silver leather menus got lengthier and lengthier and were thus considered to be nourishment in themselves. The 'Sprig of Parsley lightly dampened and served with Lemon Wedgette Natural, Sauce de Diabolo' was superb by any standards; I congratulated the beautiful Madam Chevalviande upon it, suggesting that my compliments be conveyed to her famous husband. As soon as he had completed his nightly battering, humiliation and sacking of his assistant chefs, he emerged, meat cleaver in hand, slashed wildly at Kevin the gypsy violinist and glowered savagely at his adoring habitués. His great black beard and huge hooked nose adding to his fierceness, despite his short and rotund body. There was something about his eyes that reminded me strongly of someone I once knew; I failed to place him however..... A gentle reminder to the enchanting Madam secured a rather pleasant bottle of an extremely rare old cognac to lubricate the journey home, and we left promising them a truly excellent report, 'naturellement', with an especial mention of the delicious hawkmoth mayonnaise.

Les Boules de Singe Bronzé has always had the reputation of an exciting place to dine, it being the establishment of one of the most idiosyncratic proprietor chefs, in a world not exactly known for quietness and sobriety. M. Dagobert Violentiné was considered by many to be the ultimate showman of his profession, a true virtuoso; a meal at Les Boules was invariably an occasion to remember, his Boeuf Rasputin is justly world renowned.

As we had already discovered, his two rival colleagues could be somewhat unbridled in their behaviour, but little more than might be expected of their profession. However, Dagobert was in a class of his own when it came to artistic tantrums. Indeed it was the unpredictability of these outbursts that packed the establishment to capacity every evening. Like his two rivals he spent most of his time in his kitchen or more often below in the sanctuary of his cellar, but when he did appear he would instantly and at random pick upon one of his clients. The assault could possibly be over an inappropriate choice of wine, holding a fork wrongly like the Americans, but more often simply for stirring coffee in the wrong

Plat du Jour. 1988. Hand coloured etching, 13.5 × 17.2 cm (5⅓ × 6⅘ in)

direction. To leave one scrap of his superb cooking on one's plate courted a violent and early demise. Men as well as women could be reduced to tears of disgrace and mortification for sprinkling a little salt on their already utterly perfect vegetables. His ravishing wife made little effort to calm him or indeed to sympathize with the selected victims; as far as she was concerned the great man could do no wrong and anyway that is what people had paid hundreds of francs to come and enjoy.

It was a most curious thing but this man too reminded me strongly of a former acquaintance; he, like his rivals, was short and sturdily built, but unlike the others he was clean shaven, indeed his bald head was not much more hairy than a prime cantaloupe melon. Suddenly in little more time than it takes a head waiter to add 20% corkage, I had the solution to what had been puzzling me about these three characters.

Taking what must have appeared to fellow diners as an incredible risk, I stated in a loud voice that my Concombres Farcis with Piranha Surprise tasted more like stewed cat basket. There was a deathly hush as Dagobert released his thumbs from the throat of an elderly widow who had been caught slipping superfluous mange-touts into her evening bag, and turned towards our table. The expression of utter rage on his face defied language, and the expression of language defies printing. Suffice it to say that the entire establishment including Miss Thelma Tewkes-fformwork (who no doubt feared she might be rendered companionless and thus have to pay for her own taxi) expected an apocalypse. He leaped towards our table grabbing a large carving knife on the way and stared into my face. 'Strewth Rev! What the 'ell you doin' 'ere', he said, 'You come over the wall too?'

Reverting immediately to french, and with much arm flapping and many excuses he rushed away to his kitchen.

Well that was it; all three chefs were one and the same man. The beards, moustaches, noses and glasses were donned as required. The three lovely women remained in probable ignorance and considerable luxury, and the all important cellars below (his sacred domain) were but one large den for (as I discovered) my former accomplice and colleague.

I felt I must immediately reassure him that for a consideration I would never divulge his true identity, ruin his three marvellous reputations or spoil his obviously excellent triple matrimonial arrangements, so I quietly slipped after him through the kitchens and to a door marked Privé. Down the dark steps I went and into the cellars which stretched beneath the three famed restaurants. On an old beer crate sat Bruiser Crawford whom I had not seen since our days in the kitchens at Dartmoor. I was in for 'less said the better' and he was doing a ten year stretch for G.B.H. and attempted mass poisoning.

'Allo cock,' he says. ''Ave a bit of bread and marge, an' a brown ale. For Gawd's sake don't tell the wives! Eh?'

fROgS PORN

LAUTREC—shortarse of the Arts
Earned his living painting tarts;
Two foot nothing in his socks
He did it standing on a box;
His girlfriend though, a decent sort,
Called him Toulouse but not too short.

DEGAS with his subtle palette
Did young ladies doing ballet;
He also painted home and hearth
And women sitting in the bath;
But if he felt a bit more cocky
Perhaps a race horse and its jockey.

PICASSO painted ladies fair,
And often painted ladies bare;
But just to show he didn't care
Put one eye ear and one eye there.

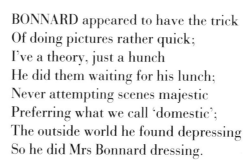

BONNARD appeared to have the trick
Of doing pictures rather quick;
I've a theory, just a hunch
He did them waiting for his lunch;
Never attempting scenes majestic
Preferring what we call 'domestic';
The outside world he found depressing
So he did Mrs Bonnard dressing.

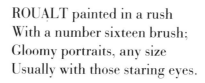

ROUALT painted in a rush
With a number sixteen brush;
Gloomy portraits, any size
Usually with those staring eyes.

SEURAT did it all with spots
And lots and lots of blinking dots;
Spotty bathers by the Seine
Just the job for painting rain.

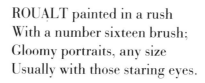

54

GAUGUIN'S work to be specific
At it's best, was quite terrific;
Lovely sets for South Pacific.

GIACOMETTI spaghetti, forgetti.

DALI really makes one feel
Inclined to go surreal;
Is there anything more soppy
Than clock and watches all gone floppy;
He counted all his surreal cash
While twiddling his real moustache.

MONDRIAN the straight line fellow
Primarily used red and yellow;
Then for something really new
Perhaps he'd do a square of blue.
Did no one tell him when at school
Rulers was against the rule?

MODIGLIANI we like much
For he has the common touch;
While without being really rude
He paints nice ladies in the nood.

What this squiggler MIRO did
Could well be painted by a kid;
Though neither clever, smart or funny
They seem to fetch a lot of money.

VAN GOGH last but not the worst
(and some of us would put him first),
Painted landscapes flat and level
Working like the very devil;
Night time cafés, old church towers
And of course that vase of flowers.
Perhaps the sun or all the strain
Did something dreadful to his brain;
Poor Vincent, such a lonely lad,
It really makes me feel quite sad;
When you think the Irises he did
Fetched more than thirty million quid.

RENOIR painted plumpish girls
With chubby chops and lustrous curls;
He could paint 'em if they'd got 'm –
Also master of the bottom.

55

Van Gogh's actual
shaving brush
also used for
priming canvases.

A la Carte. 1988. Hand coloured etching. 13.5 × 17.4 cm ($5\frac{1}{3} \times 6\frac{4}{5}$ in)

NOBLESSE OBILGE in fROGRITANIA

The writer/artist wishes to thank the owners of the following beautiful Chateaux of the Loire:

Chateau Chinon
Chateau Cheverny
Chateau Chaumont
Chateau Chambord
Chateau Chevernon
Chateau Chenonceau
Chateau Chanonmont
Chateau Chinmonsont
Chateau Chaxbarmont
Chateau Chomptouseaup
Chateau Chamverynoncence

Shatto La Trine

. . . whose gracious permission to include their exquisite dwellings in this humble work has neither been considered, sought nor refused.

POISSONERIE GORDERN BENET COQUILLAGE SUR MER

'Zee sekrat hov mar feesh spp heez non honlee ter marself, harftair eur leurftarm hov 'xpiriance has ay grert sherf du kweezeen. Bert hay weel doo may berst for owyewzay een Ngland ze Arntarn Cordiarle ernd for ze 'ducation eyer wonfeull Prins Sharles and heez lervlay warf.
Ferst yew merst 'ave ze fishs erbsolutelee frersh, zat hallmerst gers wizout sying. Bert yew werd bee sprized ow many erv mar rarvel sherfs du nert erply ziss smpl rrull, in fact eet ers drrerdfeul wert a lert of erld merde zay will cherk in.
For instarnse Dagobert Violentiné de Paris fabriceurts iz feesh spp wiz eur leurd euv eurld 'chat alimentation' erze wee say een frarnse, ers erbslootlee dsgersting...'

57

LOIRE CHATEAUX
(LEWARR SHATTOZE)

An extract from:

A Thoro Glimpse of Europe with Chuck n'Marvinette Loudengorper, Day 3
by Chuck n'Marvinette Loudengorper

'You'll simply adore this simply adorable Lewarr Valley (france)', say Chuck n' Marvinette Loudengorper. 'It's really something else charmwise.'

Once you've truly enjoyed London's adorably famous Edinburg Castle and done the Grand Canal in Rome, why not make the folks back home in Skunk Creek, Calif., real sick green by doing Europe's best kept secret, the adorable Lewarr Valley. Just brimful of fairytale castles and all built by Dooks and such simply thousands of years ago. Wow!

Check the exchange rate moneywise before renting your little auto, and haggle! It's all part of the fun! When you purchase your ticket to each Chateau (Shatto) don't forget to say 'Hey buddy, I just wanna look around some, I don't wanna buy the Goddam thing.' Say it real loud too or your little french guy just won't understand languagewise.

Although the Chateaux (Shattoze) are all pretty identical, they all have different names, and in french too. Wow! So always take a quick shot of each other standing by the name board of each and every adorable castle, so the folks back home in Skunk Creek, Calif., can't say you spoofed. Sometimes we even go inside! There is just so much culture to be gotten it's best to leave the engine running to save time.

When you've thoroughly visited twenty or thirty and it's time to take a little nourishment foodwise, as you can't find a Macdonalds why not utterly relax with some truly french cuisine (kweezeen) and take some real french wine just like the locals! Shout real clear to your waiter though, and above all don't smile or he'll take you for a real knucklebrain and overcharge pricewise.

Rest assured folks, when you're in the adorably adorable Lewarr Valley you're in real good company. For some of the truly famous have purchased dwellings here and been truly proud to call it home. Little Joan of Arc, the famous french feminist; old Dickie Lionhearted (former King of England); Cathy Medici of Medici, the Mafia Banking family and her boyfriend, Leon da Vinci (Italian artist). Even Ezard Schlumberger of Schlumberger Canine Beauty Prods. of Ohio Inc., has a little domicile hereabouts; as well as freaky french writers with names like Frankie Rabelaise and Honory De Ballsack. Check the exchange rate before buying one yourself!

Have a nice day now!

Obviously Chuck n'Marvinette, 'truly wonderful' as their travel book may be, can hardly be said to have studied the Loire Valley in great depth; but presumably they did actually go there. The same cannot be said of Attila the Hun who only got as far as Orleans, and Cecil P. Bodkin of 83a Electricity Villas, Peckham, S.E. London who only got as far as Margate. But it's certainly true of Richard the Lionheart, Catherine de Medici, and another 185 million tourists in the high season. You'll probably find these chateaux are a bit fancified for Englishmen, but not too bad considering they must have been built by the french. However it's probably their wives we really have to thank.....

 ## 1597

Scene: the sixth best drawing room at *Chateau Dupont*, six kilometres west of Tours.

LA DUCHESSE:	Henri!
LE DUC	(putting down *Le Soleil*). Oui, mon petit choufleur. Qu'est-ce que c'est cette temps?
LA DUCHESSE:	Les Jones dans le Chateau d'à côté porte avait construire un nouveau aile de l'Ouest dans le style nouveau; c'est très chic.
LE DUC:	Mon dieu! Un autre. C'est le troisième cette année, n'est pas?.
LA DUCHESSE:	Non c'est le quatrième actuellement, et c'est haut temps que nous construire une autre aile pour chez nous, vous connais. Avec tourrettes sur.
LE DUC:	Merde, un autre? Mais ce n'est pas nécessaire, c'est seulement les deux de nous, et Fifi votre poodle merdique.
LA DUCHESSE:	Ce n'est pas le point, Henri, et vous très bien connaisez cette.
LE DUC:	Eh bien, mon petit. Appeler les sanglant architects encore, rien pour un vie tranquil.

GASTRONOTE

All over france (and even in England), at least in the posher mode of restaurant, after you've been through the fairly interesting job of choosing your 'starter' and 'main course', you eventually get stuck into your gerbil and greengage soup, or canard doings avec framboisette mouselline de splodge. When this is gone (all too quickly), you hang about making bread pellets, feeling thirsty and wondering why you're not at home with your kids eating sausage and mash, when the waiter sticks a miniature sherry glass of something in the very spot you were hoping for your venison en boote avec tout les trimmings gourmandoiseière. The first time it happens it's very unnerving as you think you might have had a memory lapse and forgotten a whole main course, and that the scrapings of the deep freezer's innards have somehow got mistaken by the new under-chef for a 'dessert surprise'. Sorbet. Un-asked for, unwelcome, uneatable, stick it back in the ice bucket where it belongs.

Chez Nous. 1989. Hand coloured etching, 34.1 × 54.8 cm (13½ × 21½ in)

LES PLUS IMPORTANT
CHATEAUX de la LOIRE
EN TOUT ©

Joan of Arc

RICHARD
COUR de LION

LE FISHINGCLUB VAL DE LOIRE

Blues St Louis. 1988. Hand coloured etching, 34.4 × 27.2 cm (13½ × 10¾ in)

EAR, ACHES IN PROVENCE

Whilst visiting the bottom bit of france
In the part your actual locals call Provence,
At the chemists getting something for my cough
I meet this artist Mr. V. V. Gogh.
He'd knicked himself while shaving (so he said),
Looked more serious by the way it bled and bled.
His claim he'd done it shaving did seem weird,
Especially as he'd got a bristling beard.
Apparently he'd damaged his left lug'ole
And nearly lost a section down the plug'ole.
Incident interessant à la Pharmacie?
More like a case of arty blooming barmacy.
He's always doing that the locals said,
Poor lad's got something dodgy in his head.
The chemist said it's just the way he's made,
But never mind it brings a bit of trade.
To see him bandaged thus made me feel bad,
'What makes you do it? Why are you so sad?'
' 'Cos no one wants my paintings, Sir', he said.
They will young Vincent when you're good and dead.
You paint your lovely sunflowers while you may;
The cut-throat part will come another day.
And taking out my wallet from my blazer
I purchased him a nice new safety razor.

                                        Anon.

Apart from the anonymous writer of the foregoing poem, poor old Vincent had all
too little encouragement from his fellow men during his short working life. One has
the sneaking suspicion that dear Theo was only being brotherly in his postal
encouragements, and gently trying to con-vince Vince that he was not an utter
failure.

However, another of the items presented for my perusal by Sir Philip was the collected letters of Lady Tankerton-Foxtonsil (1831–1950), and I offer this brief extract for your consideration. It has implications of extreme importance for the present day Fine Art market, and in particular could upset the International auction houses; in fact if you have recently invested in an original Van Gogh yourself, it's probably best you don't read the next few pages at all.

THE DIARIES OF LADY TANKERTON-FOXTONSIL

ARLES
4th Aug 1888

Dear Aunt Araminta,

Just a quick note from the South of france to keep you up-to-date on your devoted niece's artistic peregrinations across the Channel.

This is the third week of our little sketching holiday in this perfectly charming part of the World. I and the dozen other members of the Plumpstead Ladies' Guild of Arts and Crafts are enjoying it immensely. Despite the various attacks of sunstroke, insects, colleywobbles and somewhat over-attentive natives of the opposite gender.

On Monday, whilst refreshing ourselves with a well-earned cup of tea in the delightful Salon du Thé (having spent an entire half hour doing 'landscape'), we became engaged in conversation with a most respectable and well-mannered young Dutchman who it transpired was a keen amateur himself, a Mr V.V.Gogh. Apparently he was on an extended working holiday here for the good of his somewhat delicate health.

There being safety in numbers and he appearing so polite, we accepted his kind offer to visit his nearby Studio; it was all most exciting. We did not take to his colleague in the same way at all however; a rather swarthy, surly personnage by the name of Paul Goggin, who appeared to be continually muttering about leaving france forever. Our arrival apparently was the last straw, and off he stormed swearing and cursing most dreadfully. Mrs Blithe-Sprakes, who understands the french language quite well, said she felt quite weak at the knees.

Considering dear Mr Gogh's kind invitation and that his friend had now departed, the least we could do was to give his little place a jolly good and much needed tidy up. To be perfectly frank, his pictures we considered a little garish and rather clumsy, while his friend's offerings (most of which we burned) perfectly hideous to say the least.

His gratitude for our ministrations was quite touching and brought tears to the dear man's eyes. He insisted on the spot that we have a free course of tuition in flower painting, and seemed so dreadfully upset when we explained that Mrs Blithe-Sprakes was conducting our tuition that we *felt obliged to concur, hence we returned the next day at 9am. Apparently he had already finished seven pictures that morning and was just applying the final daubs to a hasty portrait of the local postman who had called with a letter from his brother Theodore. Accordingly Mrs Blithe-Sprakes informed us that this style of work was known as Post Impressionism.*

Dear Mr Gogh suggested we put aside our watercolour boxes for the day, and execute a flower painting in oils. To this end he placed on the table an enormous bunch of rather tired sunflowers, but restrained our clever Miss Pletheridge from arranging them properly. He placed them in a rather awful jug which had the word Vincent painted on it. Mrs Blithe-Sprakes informed us that this was a traditional wine jug, Vincent literally meaning 'a hundred wines'.

It was quite obvious that he very much wanted us to imitate his style as closely as possible, and the more we did (it not actually being terribly difficult) the better pleased and excited he became.

Gertrude Blithe-Sprakes was obliged to admit that he was an enthusiastic and encouraging teacher, though definitely lacking a little in refinement and good taste, she suggested that if he so wished he might join us the next day in 'flower arranging Grade III' back at the Hôtel des Beaux Prix.

Alas he never arrived, and when we called to see if our paintings were dry, neither he nor they were anywhere to be found. The postman merely said he had probably had one of his funny turns again. What a shame.

Please give my regards to dear Uncle Bimbo, and my love to the dogs.

Your affectionate niece Amelia.

P.S. If you could see your way clear to dispatching another half-dozen boxes of uncle's reefers, we'd all be most grateful. A.

Menu Turistico. 1988. Hand coloured etching, 34.4 × 17.4 cm (13½ × 6⅘ in); (43.3 × 34.5 cm
(17 × 13½ in); 34.4 × 17.2 cm (13½ × 6⅘ in)

Like many an Englishman before me I would not have found it too much of a hardship to dally awhile in this South of france. There's something about it that gives one the feeling it's holiday time all the year round. Whether it's the wine or the food, or the sunshine and wine, or simply the food and wine it's hard to decide; suffice it to say that the area has much to recommend it.

However, having accompanied me thus far on my Grand Tour you will know that I am not a person to be distracted by such trifles* as food and drink. My resolve therefore, in order to follow the would-be footsteps of One Tobias, was to travel on into Italy. I planned to avoid Switzerland; I already have an excellent pocket watch, not enough cash to warrant a shady bank account and do not eat Swiss roll either within or without my trifle. But apart from all this I had read somewhere that it is a rather hilly area of Europe, and therefore not best suited to the coarse cyclist, even with Sturmey-Archer three speed gears. However a brief look at the map of Europe at the back end of my Boy's Own Diary revealed that whichever way one chose to look at it 'The Alps' (a range of mountains) lay between the bottom bit of france and the top bit of Italy. Since this present volume is not concerned with deeds of personal heroism on my part, or feats of supreme human endurance, I'll not even mention the epic crossing. For those of you who might be curious, I would simply suggest you await my book *In Hannibal's Tyremarks*; Vols. 1–49 deal with the ascent, while Vol. 50 covers the other bits including my subsequent operation in St. Brunhilda's Cycling Hospital.

Hannibal (a cannibal) and his 37 persistent pachyderms got right up the famous Roman nose by storming in through the tradesman's entrance while the Romans were having tea; all credit therefore to him and them, eh? That was in B.C. 213, so it's not possible to swap tales with good old Hannibal. We can't say with certainty who had the more difficult journey. One thing I *have* learned though is the secret of his success in trouncing the mighty legions waiting at the foot of the steps so effectively: Elephants have no brakes.

---

* In fact trifle is not one of my best loved comestibles, but seems a rather messy way to ruin a decent drop of sherry.

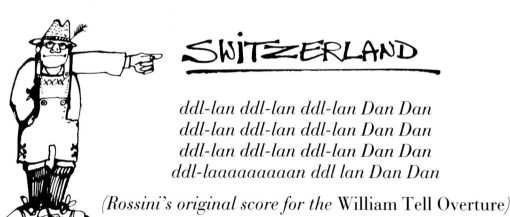

SWITZERLAND

ddl-lan ddl-lan ddl-lan Dan Dan
ddl-lan ddl-lan ddl-lan Dan Dan
ddl-lan ddl-lan ddl-lan Dan Dan
ddl-laaaaaaaaan ddl lan Dan Dan

(Rossini's original score for the William Tell Overture*)*

As we all know, old Hannibal didn't stop his long and violent rush downhill until he hit the Roman Legions; in my own case it was the Leaning Tower of Pisa.

Not surprisingly my initial reaction was to think I'd done the damage myself. However one quick glance at the millions of items on offer in the several thousand souvenir shops that cluster around the base put my mind at rest on that particular score. Any loss of verticality that the Tower displays has been there for some time and is widely regarded as an asset rather than a defect; the lean had in former times proved ideal for Galilei Galileo to dangle his doings off apparently.

Note: Pisa is in the region that the Italians are pleased to call Toscana and we are nearly as pleased to call Tuscany. Diligent readers are invited therefore to attempt an elephant joke at this point and may care to contact the publishers with it.

LEO NARDODAVINCI
PART the 1st

LORENZO:	Now look here Leonard old boy, I've a little job I want done and you're the very chap. You know that awful leaning tower they've done over at Pisa, the one that's proving such a tourist attraction?
LEONARDO:	Yes Guv. Mr Machiavelli told me.
LORENZO:	I want you to pull it down but make it look like an accident.
LEONARDO:	Erm, I've a better idea Guv. Why don't we straighten her up? More embarrassing to them as you might say.
LORENZO:	Excellent, but is it possible? And more important, would it be expensive?
LEONARDO:	It would Guv. We'd have to dig a long tunnel and buy all the lifting gear; cost you an arm and a leg as you might say.
LORENZO:	You and your anatomical drawings Leonard!

Italics. 1988. Hand coloured etching, 26.3 × 25 cm ($10\frac{1}{3}$ × $9\frac{4}{5}$ in)

EYE TIDDLY EYE TYE

In eleven hundred and seventy-three
In the Tuscan part of Italy,
Where the Arno and its torrents
Occasionally dampen Florence,
The Church though holding Catholic power
Lacked a fine and noble tower.

Said the Bishop with a smile
'We must build a campanile.
Much less chance of going to Hell
If we ring a nice big bell;
In any case it's fun as well.'

'Compared to it La Tower Eiffel
Paris, will appear a trifle;
The Empire State of New York City
Will simply seem to be a pity,
And anyway not half so pretty.'

So the clergy did select
One Isiah-architect.
'Now look 'ere lad if you are able,
Put to shame the one at Babel.'
So he drew plans upon his table.
In fact it was a sloping desk
That's why he done it 'Romanesque'.
Thus you see this clever geezer
Designed the famous Tower of Pisa.

To this day it's still not certain
Whether 'twas built behind a curtain:
For no one noticed that the dope
Had done the whole thing on the slope.
'O my God! My sainted Aunt!
He's built the damn thing on the slant.
How those Anglicans will laugh
when they read it in their Telegraph.
I rather think my Holy pardon'll
be required', said a scarlet Cardinal.
'All we can do is pray and hope',
said a nervy-looking Pope;
then crossed himself to help him cope.

'Brothers please don't moan and bicker',
Said a visiting English Vicar.
'To excommunicate is hateful,
In fact you should be rather grateful,

VIA ITALIANO

This oddity the fellow's made
Will instigate the tourist trade;
Your architect, this clever chap's
Put Pisa on the tourist maps.
Good lord you know this tower so quaint
Is better than a bloomin' Saint,
And all because it upright 'aint.'

'So this tower though fantastic'll
Fill our coffers ecclesiastical.
Now we comprehend the meaning
Of this tower's curious leaning.
He really is a clever devil
For any town could have one level.
Any fool could build one plumb
But we in Pisa ain't so dumb –
It's like a static pendulum.
Who wants a load of Florence churches
When Pisa's got a tower that lurches?
What name hast thou? For we must know
In order honours to bestow.'

'They call me One Isiah, brother,
'Cos one eye's 'igher than the other,
(Quite upsetting for my Mother).
The world all seems cock-eyed you see,

What's straight for you just 'aint for me.
And I confess it's been my passion
To do a building in this fashion.
To me the tower is straight and true
Though I know it looks all odd to you;
But I never meant to bring disgrace
Or put a carbuncle on the face
Of such a great and noble place.
Please tell me it's O.K. your Grace.'

One Isiah (Architect)

'We understand', the Pope proclaimed,
'And indeed you'll not be blamed,
For Pisa now's forever famed,
And from its most unusual angle,
On Mondays we can washing dangle.
We like the style of this new-fangle.
To celebrate this great surprise
And since I've praised you to the skies,
Nip off and get some Pisa pies!'

73

THE PONTY JOB

It's all too obvious during your wanderings round Florence that the Ponte Vecchio is almost entirely occupied by goldsmiths, diamond merchants, jewellers and suchlike stalwarts of honest travail; one of the many 'nice little earners' dreamed up by the Medici Corp. in times gone by. A generous slice of the financial action to the 'firm' and you get a prime spot on the Ponte. This is all history but the evidence is still there.

What is less well known but not too surprising though, is that this was also the site of the world's largest robbery. Well it would have been had the fates been kinder to our hero. Had his brilliant plan succeeded he would have instantly become the richest man in the world; the Czar of Russia having to take a poor second place. In due course he would also have earned the undying gratitude of film producers the world over. Lord Sidcup Bypass was not his real name of course (although he did come from that interesting area of S.E.London) but he could affect the manner of an aristocrat, certainly well enough to convince the average foreigner. It was towards the end of the last century when nearly everybody (except the french) still had proper Kings, Queens and Royal families to their credit.

It was the night before the Gritti Palace Coming Out Party. This annual event attracted all the crown heads of Europe* together with Viscountesses, Duchesses, Princesses and all the aristocratic young ladies who wished to join their ranks, and all on the look out for the right young chap to make it happen.

The shopkeepers on the Ponty did a roaring trade, not only selling new items and spiving up the old, but also holding all valuables in safe-keeping prior to their adorning the nubility the next evening.

All these fine personages were far too excited to listen to the weather forecast on the soon to be invented Marconi wireless.

His Lordship who had actually only popped over to Florence on the look out for a fabulously wealthy Princess or two (he was, as you realize, what we call a bit of a cad), hearing that there was to be heavy rain, suddenly formed an incredible plan. He purchased (on borrowed money naturally) every coal barge on the entire River Arno, and stealthily parked them tight as enormous sardines beneath the three great arches of the old bridge. Don't ask me why the goldsmiths didn't notice, perhaps they were all drunk or at a Mafia Ladies' Night Do; anyway everyone else was at the hairdresser without exception.

Towards midnight His Noble Lordship waited anxiously for the promised deluge and consequent rise in water level. Had the weather forecasters got it wrong yet again? He considered other methods of adding liquid to the river such as buying a round of drinks for the local football team, but there was no time. Mother nature had 'worked a dreadful flanker' on him and the Arno failed to flood.

Exactly what his plans were had the bridge been lifted sufficiently to snap off at the ends and glide downstream on its raft of barges we shall never know.

The disappointment was all too much for the young man, however, and he 'went wrong' as it's called, going from bad to worse and eventually becoming an estate agent just like his father.

* All except Queen Victoria of course.

Fresco Oggi. 1989. Hand coloured etching, 13.5 × 17.4 cm (5⅓ × 6⅘ in)

THE RENUISANCE MAN

i t's surprising how many people don't realize that this place in it's day was something of a centre for artiness, etc. Some would even go so far as to say a 'cultural hub'. Just like Biggleswade is today and to a lesser extent Paris or Athens were in their time.

If you think the french use their hands rather a lot when in conversation, just wait till you see the Italians; it's wonderful to behold, and every conversation looks and sounds like a full-scale row. Though they are probably only having a little chat about how mild the weather is for October, it sounds as though one has just strangled the other's granny. Both parties appear to regard their opposite number as an utter imbecile. Just as you are looking forward to seeing the physical violence, the whole thing disappointingly peters out and they cheerily go their separate ways as though nothing had happened – funny old lot.

LINGUANOTE

LORENZO FLORENZO

(I'll maka ze doors Uffizi windows)

Ringed around with pale blue mountains
Sprinkled by a thousand fountains,
There's this place Italiano
By a river called the Arno,
Norm'ly flowing quite *piano*;
And long before the days of Rome
Etruscans called it 'home sweet home'.
'Everytime we cross this river,
We get wet feet and tend to shiver.
So being fairly clever chaps
Let's put on our thinking caps,
And measure where it's not too wide
To build a bridge from side to side.'
But suddenly one rainy day
The whole damn lot got washed away.

Florence gained her famous name
Much later when the Romans came.
So smartly dressed in tin and leather
(With sandals during milder weather),
They bravely marched in soldier's gear
And clipped the locals round the ear.
The governmenti Roman style
Was status quo for quite a while.
Then humble people raised their hopes
When Romans started having popes;
Christian slaves were all set free,
Instead of making Lions' tea.

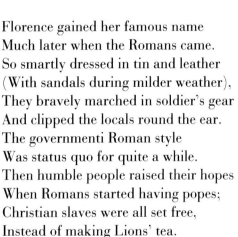

Then Florence thrived and grew and grew,
And so did merchants' purses too;
I doubt if there's a place more sunny
Where such chaps ever made such money.
Did you know the wealth of Florence
Came from banking and insurance?
So building started with a burst,
Much pleasing Cosimo the First.
'Now that I've got all this power
I'm going to need a great stone tower,
And at the populace I'll glower
As I sit and watch my Florence flower.'

It's a Doge's Life on the Grand Canal. 1988. Hand coloured etching, 54.3 × 68.9 cm (21⅜ × 27 in)

And with his rivals full of malice,
He strengthened his Uffizi Palace;
For even in this land of plenty
There were still some Malcontenti.
They wanted rich Medici's money —
And with his stack that wasn't funny.
Now every townsman Florentine
Was either Guelph or Ghiberline;
All the city's nastier actions
Involved the warring of these factions;
Expressions of the utmost hate
Concerning votes for Pope or State.
But being nervous of the rain
Since flooding caused them so much strain,
Even in a gentle shower
They'd be half way up the bloody tower.

The next Medici, name of Lawrence
Really changed the face of Florence;
Gave them civic pride, and so
They called him 'Il Magnifico'.
'Let sculptor sculpt, and painter paint
Fine frescos here of every Saint;
Paint them on the still wet plaster
So you can do 'em even faster.'
And thus began the golden age
When artists took the centre stage,
(Some even earned a living wage).
The monkish ones were unpaid though
Such as Fra Angelico;
He worked because he loved his Master
Content with justa bowla pasta.

Lorenzo in a speech impassioned
Declared all rival towns 'old fashioned'.
'I find that Pisa quite grotesque
With its so called Romanesque;
Brunelleschi he's the fella
Fran-chesco'd by young Piero della;
Medici needed no convincing
Using much Leon da Vincing —
Decorating church and mission
With art by Raphael and Titian, who
When painting in his colours mellow,
Occasionally ran short of yellow;
So pinched a tube off nice Uccello
'Donatella Donatello'.

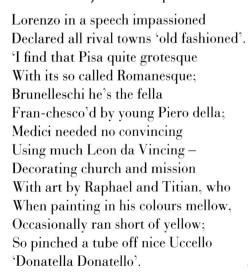

And when the artwork went too slow
Lawrence phoned Michelangelo.

'Do us another statue Mike',
And he'd dash over on his bike;
And all about results you'll see
Of Firenzed activity.

Now come on workers don't be lazy
I want it big like Piranese;
A bit more effort you can hoista
Damn great stone to builda cloister.
A belltower will impress the people
And don't forget a decent steeple,
For with a great big pointed spire
You'll get it looking even higher.
Now look 'ere lad, I don't care how high
Just put the top bit near the sky.'
So Florence, done with past complacence,
Set in motion The Renaissance;
Though architectural styles got garbled
When later on the fronts were marbled.
'O mercy me it looks like rain,
Move your feet you'll block that drain.'

Lorenzo told 'em with a shout
(And doubtless waving arms about),
'Get your paints and brushes out;
Get to work, impress the nation,
Earn yourself a reputation;
Paint those frescos, carve that stone,
Raise the roof and raise the tone;
Do a decorated frieze
Bring in the Yanks and Japanese;
Must get rid of Sav'narola,
I've a yen for coca-cola;
O God our help in ages past
Please bring in the dollars, fast.'

'Who forgot to say his prayers?
There's water creeping up the stairs!
O God above we pray deliver
No extra liquid in our river;
When molto fiatsa in the Piazza
And all them carsa in the Plazza;
To gain our everlasting thanks
Make Arno stay within its banks.'
'Hold on now Sir', said good St. Francis,

81

'I don't think you've got all the answers;
Great artists made this place with love
To glorify our God above;
Your motives hardly are the purist,
You're only thinking of the tourist.'

'Quite frankly, if I might be frank,
People call you Frank the Crank.
They say you've only built your church
So 'brother pigeon's' got a perch;
To men like me it seems absurd
To fork out cash on just a bird.'
'I assure you, Sir, the humble pigeon
Has much to do with true religion;
For symbolized by lowly dove,

Our Lord above is God of Love
To everything beneath his skies,
Whether it swims or crawls or flies.'
'All very nice', said dubious Lawrence,
'I prefer a cash-based Florence.'

In every shop in every strada
Are works resembling Leonarda;
Wonderful for he who seeks
To purchase priceless new antiques;
Or when you've scoffed down your risotto
And slept it off inside a grotto,
Buy yourself a nice Giotto.

And you'll discover walking round
That statues of the nude abound;
Great big ladies, forms 'divine'
On settees made of stone recline;
Chubby cherubs, a cheeky cupid,
Grecian heroes looking stupid;
They doubtless feel a wee-bit silly,
Big Hercules and Little Willy?
Never mind, we'd best not moan
They're 'cultural', these lumps of stone.

Though evidence is somewhat scanty
I'm told this was the home of Dante,
Who writ his comedy divine
In joined-up writing, line by line;
Then he signed it 'Yours infernal'
And thus he made his name eternal;
But whether masterpiece or hoax,
For us discerning English blokes
As 'comedy', its short on jokes.

PART the 2nd

MICHELANGELO: 'Allo, what you working on now then Leon?

LEONARDO: Book about Steadman, Mike actually. So keep your beadies off it.

MICHELANGELO: It's a good idea, Leon. Wish I'd thought of it myself. Don't worry, I can't read your writing anyway. It looks all back to front. What you going to call it?

LEONARDO: Thought I'd call it 'I Ralpho'. But don't tell no one or I'll dissect you.

MICHELANGELO: Nice one Leon. I 'spect your going to do lots of drawings and that for it, eh?

LEONARDO: Might...

MICHELANGELO: Oooh! What's that daft-looking machine over there? You're always making daft-looking machines Leon.

LEONARDO: That's a Bugatti seven-speed racing car gear-box.

MICHELANGELO: No, not that one, the funny thing next to it.

LEONARDO: Oh, that's an automatic splodge-nib-buster and ink squirt; with such a clever device absolutely anybody can do a Steadman picture. Mind you, you've got to be a brilliant draughtsman to start with.

MICHELANGELO: Wow Leon! Let's have a go.....

LEONARDO: Sorry Mike, I said brilliant draughtsmen only.

TAKING UMBRIAGE in TUSCANY

I'm ashamed to have to admit this but ever since the refurbishment of 'Cherry View', the row of sturdy council houses in our village at home in Kent, I've been a bit 'iffey' concerning buildings done in red brick. Can't really explain why.

Pretty well the whole of Siena is reddish brick except the cathedral which is a goody by any standards and is in horizontal 'get to heaven faster' stripes of black and white marble.

Mind you they were pretty good brickies on our council houses, and I must admit the ones in Siena and environs all those years ago weren't bad either. Masters of the trade so to speak; in fact I've read in a learned work written by someone who not only ought to know better but probably does, that your Sienese bricklayer was in great demand Europewide for quite a time.

I'm a wood and stone man myself, as indicated, but I am obliged to give credit where credit is due.

It's got a wonderful Town Hall has Siena, called quite rightly the Palazzo Pubblico in front of which is a large paved area which most cities would cherish as a fine and noble car park. Not so your crafty Sienese Town Council, they use it as a circuit for horse races and thereby make themselves into a world famous tourist attraction, and the odd billion lire.

Tuscany is positively riddled with fine old buildings in fine old towns perched on the top of fine old hills growing fine old grapes for Chianti so you can have a fine old hangover. Mooching about these places you'll soon realize that everything, although quite obviously ancient, remains in what we the cognoscenti refer to as 'fairly good nick'.

This is surprising as the good natured folk of Tuscany have spent the last two thousand years trying to knock each other's towns and cities into a pile of rubble.

One would like to think that whatever it was in the Tuscan temperament that made them so spiteful to each other in the past, it was now out of their system. Largely true, I'm pleased to say.

The last vestiges of this are to be seen however in their own brand of Antica Footballo Hooliganismi in which they dress up in ridiculous Medieval Costumes and bash the living daylights out of each other. I just thought you might be interested.

84

St. Francis. 1988. Hand coloured etching, 29.1 × 21.2 cm (11½ × 8⅓ in)

I'LL BE A MONKEY'S UNCLE

I'll bet there's more than a few of my revered readers who (like me) have always imagined hagiography to be the study of Scotsmen, and therefore given it an accordingly wide berth. In fact nothing could be further from the truth, it's actually the exact opposite. Hagiography is the study of Saints.

Finding myself in the enchanting little city of Assisi, I decided to do a little hagiographizing myself and check up on this St. Francis character. Apparently he was a man of some influence as he appeared to be responsible not only for the several thousand or so thriving gift and souvenir shops and a dozen beautiful churches, but also the bus service, car parks, betting shop, greengrocers and grappa distillary. In fact it was difficult to find anything in the entire Assisi area which did not wish to associate itself in some way with the holy personage. You don't normally have this kind of success just by being kind to animals, so there must have been something else about him. There was.

He was we find far more interested in following the example of Christ than in being merely religious, and as a consequence much more interested in being simply good and kind than holy. There's no reason to suppose he ever wanted to be a Saint at all. But there you are, a year or two after he died they made him into one, and in some sense spoiled everything. Still at least he was the kind of chap to get Saints a good name, he even had a nice girlfriend by the way.

O DEAR ST. FRANCIS

O Dear St. Francis, looking down
At trade within your holy town;
D'you wonder in the way we do
If shopkeepers give thanks for *you*;
For over several hundred years
They've coined a bit from souvenirs.
Do any, taking stock each day
Get down upon their knees and pray,
'O God above it's Thee we thank
For all this cash and *good old Frank*;
For Lord without your lovely monk
We couldn't flog this dreadful junk.'

No. Let's be full of charity,
Say O! yes, yes, or Ah! Si, Si.

NOFTI
(Notes for the Interested)

As indicated in the little poem, I was not too impressed with the articles for sale in the Religioso Giftatti shops of Assisi. Some of the cheap little ceramic copies of ancient and beautiful crucifixes were acceptable and the postcards of them, and other wonderful Mediaeval works. But there seemed little produced in the last few centuries with what might be called sincerity, let alone design and craftmanship.

Herewith my attempt at something better.

I must confess, my seven-year-old, Tilly, helped even more than usual with this picture. Naturally her personal guinea pig was of particular importance, but she also provided vital information on our other various family pets, both alive and 'no longer amongst us' too. Happy the Pony (famous for not kicking people), Snibbo, Speckledy Ned and the 500 kittens. Lambsy and No. 16, those most affectionate of sheep, as well as Jason's Minah bird, Strawberry (not Morris). And our dogs past and present: Labrador Mima, songstress and food burglar; Daffy, absolutely genuine Kentish Cathound; and Jessie, an 'obediance trial' if ever there was one.

Francis himself takes centre stage and is seen with some of his own animal friends, including the fierce wolf of the well-known legend. I don't want to knock good old St. Francis, but it could be that the wolf was coming to the end of his rampaging Mafia days anyway, and simply wanted a quiet life and a bit of respectability. No, Frank was the real thing alright. Actually, it's possible he might not have really been all that religious. He might have been just a Christian — much more difficult of course, but far more in tune with all God's birds and animals.

Molto Economico. 1989. Hand coloured etching, 13.5 × 17.3 cm (5⅓ × 6⅘ in)

IT'S A DOGE'S LIFE ON THE GRAND CANAL

Dear reader, as you well know when you're book reading (as long as it's not Hebrew, Chinese or Japanese), the number of pages held in the left hand gradually increases while those in the right reduce in number unless you are one of those disgraceful persons who flick through books from the back, in which case you've not been reading this but merely gawping at the pictures anyway.

By applying the simple test aforementioned, you will be sad or glad to realize that we are approaching the end of this present volume. Having loyally read, peddled and staggered with me this far, dear reader, there is some sad news I have to impart regarding Venice.

In general we are more than happy with this place, for although far from home, it is all oddly but pleasantly familiar. Probably due in most cases to devout perusal of the works of Canaletto and M. Cruddy R.A. in Boots or W.F.Woolworth's Fine Art depts., framed and found gilty at £9.95. City of a myriad ice cream commercials and assorted biscuit tins, Venice is justly world famous. But apart from all this rather obvious visual charm, who actually put Venice 'on the map' so to speak? This brings me to the bitter news, the terrible disgrace, the undeniable evidence just goes to prove how people from other countries are foreigners through and through. There is not one statue of William Shakespeare in the whole blooming city! Venice's greatest benefactor totally ignored.

There is nothing – not so much as a rude graffiti round the back of the Rialto post office cycle sheds. And that's another thing! There are no cycle sheds; cycles are apparently entirely banned from Venice's streets. Another deadly insult to the English! Not a single statue to the immoral bard and I'm not allowed to ride my bike and caravan into St. Mark's Square, the ultimate goal of my whole Tour! Is it something they have against bald men with beards? Jealousy perhaps?

Thus I was forced to pursue my wanderings on foot and by boat and what with the number of bars, the generally pleasant nature of the people and the bars etc., I soon forgave Venice for its neglect of 'our chap'; they probably meant no harm, just ignorance...can't help being Italian...etc., etc.

The procedure of this forgiving process was thrown into violent reverse gear by my bumping into the statue of a poetically garbed personnage with the preposterous name of Carlo Goldini. On questioning my Venetian Informant,* I was told that this

* See Venetian Informant.

CARLO GOLDONI

Goldini was a 'famous' Italian playwright and indeed was considered by many of his more imaginative or gullible countrymen to be the 'Italian Shakespeare'! O dear, O dear, O dear, not only does he have this simpering statue in his honour, but the whole adjacent square and the daily millions walking by are obliged to smirk at him in grateful admiration.

Did this Goldini ever sit down to write 'The Two Gentlemen of Bognor', I ask, or more relevant, 'The Merchant of Chelmsford'? Not a bit of it, too busy buying silly hats with great feathers sticking out and posing for sculptors no doubt.

* My Venetian Informant. It's probably best, all things considered, that I don't reveal this good man's name. Suffice it to say he's British (well Welsh actually, but none the worse for that) and has lived in Venice since the lire was worth leering at. Knows practically everything worth bothering about when it comes to things Venetian, and speaks the language like a gondolier's grandpa.

To him I dedicate this poem:

A thars Glimpse of Europe with Chuck 'n Marinette Loudengorper (Day 4.)

Hi! Disneyville Italian style,
We're gonna visit you awhile;
Gee! What does this guide book say?
Thursday! Venice! Half a day!
Tinnereddo? My, O My!
Jeeze!, his goddam angels fly;
Now! havin' gotten culture in,
Gimme a vermoooth, ice n'gin;
I guess before we go back home,
We'd better go check out this Rome.

It's a Doge's Life on the Grand Canal

It seems a bit odd having to thank a rather offensive chap like Attila the Hun and his belligerent associates for such a beautiful place as Venice – but it's a fact.

One Monday morning a long time ago, the peacable dwellers splodging around the northern shores of the Adriatic had a ponder and came to a decision. The best way to avoid the unwelcome attentions of these Huns, Goths, Visigoths and Lombard hordes was to build a nice new place complete with a St. Mark's Square etc. on some rather wobbly islands out in the nearby Laguna. Silly it must have seemed at the time, but in practice it turned out to be one of the best ideas anyone has ever had.

Fifteen hundred years later I'm here to check up: Venice is wonderful; mind you, it's not short on Huns, Goths, Visigoths and Lombard hordes, let alone citizens of Skunk Creek, Calif. Anyway, herewith my etching to commemorate the occasion.

More news from the Rialto later.

ACQUA LITERATI

It becomes obvious as you toddle round Venice's busy streets or squash aboard their crowded waterbuses that it is, to say the least, an extremely popular place for Grand Tourists of all Nations; and it has been thus for more than a few centuries.

The list of famous visitors to Venice is almost endless, and many have been so taken with it that they've stayed on to gather their wits or ply their trade. It's curious, but Venice hasn't had too many of it's own native sons and daughters who've achieved fame. The exceptions are Perspectivo Canaletto of course (clever old stick); that obnoxious Goldini character, if you can call that 'fame'; Antonio 'Four Seasons' Vivaldi who, we learn, taught violin and singing in a sort of convent for young ladies of a wayward disposition; and that rascal who would have taken more than full advantage of the same type of work himself, Casanova 'the Bedroom Rover'.

Amongst the famous Grand Tourists have been many from our own favoured Isles, as it's been especially popular with us jolly old English. One such was no less a personage than St. Charles Dickens, and in the following extract (supposedly taken from one of his notebooks), he mentions several others.

'Hello again, this is your very own Charlie Dickens from the famous Rialto Commentary Box, bringing you the very latest in this year's Aqua Literati *gondola race.*
I've a marvellous view straight down the Grand Canal almost as far as the notorious Accademia Corner. It's a little blustery today, with the water

Lord Byron (himself)

just a little choppy, so we won't be expecting a repeat of last year's record-breaking times on this particular occasion.... But hold on, what's this?! Yes it's the first boat already rounding the last bend. My goodness, this is exciting. Yes, it's one of ours, I think. England's B team, namely Byron, Byshe Shelley and Browning. What a crew they make; they really are setting a cracking pace. But there's another boat right on their tail. Yes! I think it's the famous french philosophers' D team, Descartes, Diderot and de Rochefoucauld, but in some kind of trouble....it looks to me as though fighting has broken out.... O dear, they've smashed into the Palazzo Corner Spinelli and sunk. Never mind, I can see our artists' team entering the home straight now. In fine style too, with John Ruskin at the helm as usual, Sir Mervyn Cruddy RA, and of course Mr Wishy Washy himself, J.W.M. (or is it W.M.J?, I can never remember) Turner.

Well, well, well, England one and two, this really is a turn up for the books! And no one else yet in sight. What's happened to Richard Wagner, J.W.V. Goethe and young Gustav Mahler's boat, I wonder? Meanwhile Ruskin, Cruddy and Turner are approaching the Pallaza Papadopoli and gaining fast. I'm afraid our Lord Byron, pink silk shirt flying in the breeze, is too busy waving to the crowds...Ah! He's spotted them and the poets are putting on a spurt. Is it too late? It's almost neck and neck now as the two boats pass the San Sylvesto waterbus stop, and the Venetian crowd are going absolutely mad! What a race! Yes, I think the artists are going to win! Yes, they're under the bridge now! Well, well, well, the English artists have beaten our fine team of poets by a short erm....er..One of those funny sticking-up bits on the front of a gondola. O sod it, I've dropped my pen in the canal.

Charles Kevin Dickens

EXPRESSO EXTORTIONATO

Yes you're absolutely right. These waiters working the cafés around St. Mark's Square really are specially chosen and trained by the Mafia. At a 'college' far away in Sicily the lads are carefully selected for this most highly regarded of professions. Obviously some of them, finding they don't have the stomach for it, fall by the wayside and become mere vice racketeers or gangland bosses, the 'toughies' though serve us our drinks.

By now you'll be well aware that in many of the bars and cafés of Garibaldiland you are obliged to pay at the cash desk before actually getting to grips with your victuals, not here though or the system would be rumbled before the big pay off.

Once you've gained your waiter's attention it won't take too long to acquire a pleasing little still-life of coffee cups, Peroni beer bottles and empty grappa glasses

"yes Nous Gesprechen Ici Inglese per favore Sir"

on your table. In addition you might well have been treated to the sebaceous lilt of the quintet striking up, and so this may well seem the appropriate moment to exit stage left for a boat ride.

Suddenly Big Luigi looms bearing a small white bus ticket on a large silver tray. Printed in pale mauve on the ticket is what appears to be a rather lengthy telephone number, prodigious even for lire which are far worse than sprats when it comes to individual items per pound. It will doubtless be a great temptation to explain to your Luigi that you did not intend to purchase the actual table and chairs, and much as we all might look forward to the early retirement of his oleate skiffle group, we did not wish to commit ourselves at this stage to providing the gold watches. One merely wished to enjoy an agreeable (albeit piccolo proportioned) quaff amidst the otherwise charming Venetian hoi polloi.

But don't be tempted. 'Renumerato non hesitato', or it could be the worse for you; i.e. concrete boots and a swift shove off the Accademia bridge in the small hours, or a 'little gondola trip' as they probably call it.

You wouldn't be the first to meet this watery end. An actual Doge was drowned sometime ago, and all he did apparently was to suggest that the coffee cups were just a bit on the thick side in Florian's Cafe.

Oldest Coffee House in Europe? I should think it would be. It's hardly going to prove a non-survivor or commercial failure with a captive clientele at these kind of prices, with or without the orchestral supplemento of L.4000 per tune up.

Don't be distressed. You're not being robbed. In fact you're assisting one of the most worthwhile causes imaginable. You're actually helping to prevent poor old Venice from sinking lagoonwards for ever. Who's going to stand by and let that happen without a fight when there's this kind of money to be made just from serving a few drinks, certainly not your Mafioso.

RISING DAMPO IN THE CAMPO

O golden-oldie by the Med.,
You're slowly sinking so they say;
Tired maybe but far from dead
And smiling bravely all the way.

'Well done', Town Councillors of Venice
To chuck out all those motor cars;
You've banished mankind's four wheeled menace
So made more room for boats and bars.

Just cruising down to St. Mark's Square
In water buses molto handy;
Can there be cityscape more fair
Than that along your Canal Grande?

Yes, lovely Lily and Laguna
I rather wish I'd met you sooner.

DAMP ENDING

The banishment of the motor car from Venice is of course one of the reasons why it remains so lovely and feels so friendly. Banning the bike, however, is not friendly, especially in my own particular case, I'm bound to say.

As is well known to all, transport within the city has to be largely by water whether it's wine, fruit and veg, people (dead or alive), bricks or builders' rubbish. The result is a wonderful array of different craft. But not every Venetian has a front door opening immediately on to a canal, so goods must be moved from building to boat and vice versa. This task is undertaken by porters with huge barrows, specially adapted to climb the steps over the bridges. Almost as much a part of the Venetian scene as the gondoliers themselves, and far more useful. Nimbly swerving through the crowds of dawdling tourists, they clear their path by honking vigorously in imitation of real lorries. Rarely so much as clipping the odd pedestrian, they are masters of their trade. It's not a cheap way to get your luggage carried a few hundred yards, but it's effective.

So if these vehicles are allowed on the streets, surely my caravan might squeak through the regulations too. If I detached the forbidden bike, it might be pulled by hand; the stepped bridges would be a struggle but by no means an insuperable one. With the aid of an extra after supper grappa, one particular evening a little determination overcame much apprehension.

Now, my bike has a sturdy iron stand which, when stationary, can be folded down from beneath the huge front basket. This device, in the vertical position, renders the whole conveyance remarkably stable. With the bicycle removed, however, the caravan having no braking system of its own, becomes a wandering, wayward thing only under control when led like a dog by its towbar. When parked on any kind of slope, however gentle, it requires bricks (carried for the purpose) against the wheels to keep it in one place. In fact it is so mobile that gravity takes over at the least inclination.

Who (or what) silently removed my own carefully placed bricks that night is not known. A jealous rival art-historian perhaps? Carlo Goldini's ghost? A keen nocturnal brick enthusiast, unexpectedly finding a couple of 'Kentish stocks' to add to his collection?

I was just settling for the night when I felt the first unmistakable motions of my conveyance over the stone flags. Instinct told me to leap forth with all available agility before I and my caravan were lost forever in the murky waters. It came to an abrupt halt as we met a low stone parapet, but my act of leaping was now in full flight and could not be cancelled. Even as I travelled the few feet through the night air, I recalled One Tobias and Black Sydney; the waters did indeed seem uncommonly cold for late May...

Trattoria Romantica. 1989. Hand coloured etching, 13.5 × 17.2 cm (5⅓ × 6⅘ in)

"The Streets of Rome and Wondrous Marble Paths
remind me much of Bolton Public Baths."

Albert P. Cleghwistle
(1872 – 1987)

Albert Cleghwistle

POSTSCRIPT

A Message from St. Brunhilda's Cycling Hospital

'Allo Doc, it's only me   (Jan. 1989).
I've not been quite myself you see;
I've been off touring on my bike
And done myself a mischief, like.'
'Good Lord!', he said, 'You stupid man,
With grocer's bike and caravan!
Take them boots and trousers orf
'Op on that couch and 'ave a corf.'

'Corf, corf!' I went and he said, 'Coo,
I think I know what's wrong with you.
Crikey Clarkie, this'll learn yer
You've been an' gorn an' got a hernia.'
'Blimey Doc!', I said, 'Tut, tut!
D'you mean I've gorn and bust a gut?'
'I'm bound to tell you at this juncture,
Your Grand Tour's given you a puncture;
Not a puncture of the bike,
More of the guts and gizzards like.
And this one is sufficient bad
It's 'ospital for you old lad.'

I've had me 'op, I've been stitched up,
I've drunk me tea (well half a cup);
My lovely surgeon by some quirk
Won prizes for her needlework;
I've done with feeling 'slightly queasy'

And am prepared to 'take things easy'.
In fact I'm feeling rather fine
(They do allow a glass of wine);
So please inform the Queen and Nation
'Clarke's survived his operation'.

When mended I'll be off again
This time to Greece or maybe Spain;
Dear Wendy wife allaying fears
Has bought a bike with eighteen gears;
Lest you should think I might recapture
This first fine and careless rapture.

The End